RESUMES FOR THE HEALTH CARE PROFESSIONAL

RESUMES FOR THE HEALTH CARE PROFESSIONAL

Kim Marino

John Wiley & Sons, Inc.

New York • Chichester • Brisbane • Toronto • Singapore

In recognition of the importance of preserving what has been
written, it is a policy of John Wiley & Sons, Inc., to have
books of enduring value published in the United States
printed on acid-free paper, and we exert our best efforts
to that end.

Copyright © 1993 by John Wiley & Sons, Inc.

All rights reserved. Published simultaneously in Canada.

Just Resumes® is a registered trademark by Kim Marino.

Library of Congress Cataloging-in-Publication Data

Marino, Kim, 1951–
    Resumes for the health care professional / by Kim Marino.
        p. cm.
        Includes index.
      ISBN 0-471-55862-1 (paper : alk. paper)
      1. Resumes (Employment)   2. Medical personnel—Vocational
guidance.   I. Title.
      [DNLM: 1. Health Occupations.   2. Job Application.   W 21 M337r]
    R690.M333   1992
    610'.69—dc20
    DNLM/DLC
    for Library of Congress   91-44718

Printed in the United States of America

10 9 8 7 6 5 4 3 2 1

Preface

As the founder of Just Resumes® and author of three resume books, including *Just Resumes*® (John Wiley & Sons, October 1991), I am readily acquainted with the resume needs of health care professonals. My own files contain resume samples from a wide range of health care professionals, allowing me to stay in touch with this dynamic field and bring this knowledge to bear in the present volume.

Resumes for the Health Care Professional includes more than 100 samples of a full range of health care resumes from registered nurses to technologists and technicians to therapists and social workers to medical record technicians. Both traditional and newly created positions are addressed. This sensible step-by-step guide for creating a professionally designed resume, contains many examples from my vast bank of health care resumes. I have also included valuable inside tips and suggestions, most of which are specific to the health care field.

The book provides samples of a cover letter and thank you letter as well as how-to information to complete the resume packet. Later chapters offer a job and interview tips section that covers specific key health care jobs and descriptions of those jobs, a section on the job trends, and a detailed section on job search techniques. Chapter 9 includes more than 25 tough questions most asked in a hospital interview. And the kinds of answers the interviewer wants to hear! I also give you seven key questions to ask the hospital interviewer.

Whether you're a health care professional returning to the workforce, changing careers, or moving up, or you're a college student or recent graduate entering the health care industry, I am confident this book is one of the best investments you'll ever make.

KIM MARINO

Fort Collins, Colorado
December 1992

Acknowledgments

First I'd like to thank my editor, Mike Hamilton, who is brillant and wonderful to work with. I'd also like to express my gratitude to the following health care professionals who have been instrumental in helping me with my research in health care: my very good friend Fred Wilson, M(ASCP); Dana Clark, Director of Nurses, Olsten Health Care Services, Santa Barbara, CA; Frances Passman, Medical Technologist Supervisor at the Colorado State University Student Health Center; Dick Christensen, RN, Recruiter; Carole Trask, Assistant Human Resource Director; Marye Sweet, Human Resource Interviewer; Susan Milligan, Patient Education Coordinator; Ruth Lytle-Barnaby, LCSW, Supervisor of Medical Social Work; Stacey Scattergood, EEG Technologist; and all the many staff members at Poudre Valley Hospital in Fort Collins, Colorado.

K.M.

Contents

Contents

RESUMES FOR THE HEALTH CARE PROFESSIONAL

1

The Professional Resume

Since I started helping professionals write their resumes, I have found that health care professionals take a tremendous amount of pride in themselves and their work. But because their work is so much a part of their very existence, they are modest when it comes to telling people all the wonderful things they do for others. Health care professionals find their job rewarding and fulfilling just doing it. Does this sound familiar to you? It is especially true for the nursing profession. Remember, while preparing your resume, this is not the time to be humble. This is where you get credit where credit's due.

A resume is something you should have in your back pocket, ready to give out at a moment's notice. Why? Because you'll never know when that special job opportunity may open up for you. Your resume is a custom designed, self-marketing tool tailored to your career objectives. A professional resume functions in four ways.

1. It focuses the interviewer's attention on *your* strongest points.
2. It gives you full credit for all your achievements, whether you were paid or not.
3. It guides the interviewer toward positive things to talk about in *you*, and in the direction you want to go.
4. Most importantly, it lets *you* see yourself in a more focused and positive manner so that you become in control of your own future.

It's also the first link between you and the potential employer. (No wonder there's so much pressure on job seekers to create an effective resume!)

Many of the resumes in this book are from actual health care professionals who have been clients of Just Resumes®. Others were created for this book with accurate job descriptions and educational requirements. Let these resumes stand as examples of the kind of resume that you, with the help of this book, are going to create. Many of these clients came to me with skills and education similar to yours. Working with them, I was able to produce a personalized resume that genuinely reflected their needs, accomplishments, and goals.

Now before you leap into the resume writing process, please take a few minutes to obtain an overview of my approach to creating a professional resume. Read the first two chapters ("The Professional Resume" and "The No-Nonsense Approach to Resume Writing"). You might be tempted to jump into writing your resume at this point, but take an additional couple of minutes to read any of the next group of chapters that might apply to you. Chapter 3 describes those of you returning to the workforce after several years' absence. In Chapter 4, you'll find information on changing careers or moving up in the field you are in. And Chapter 5 offers suggestions for the recent graduate. If you haven't done so already, next turn to the resume samples in Chapter 11 to see how all the theory behind resume writing has been turned into fact.

Reading the introductory chapters and surveying actual resumes will prime you for writing your own resume. You will also want to begin analyzing your own background and pinpointing your targeted career. What you have done in previous positions or gained through education and what you want to do in your career will also influence the resume format you are going to use. You might go with the traditional chronological format, which highlights your jobs. You may wish to emphasize your skills by using the highly flexible functional format. Or you may opt to create a combination of the chronological and functional formats, which is a way of highlighting a specific job while also indicating other previous jobs. Let my step-by-step instructions and examples prompt and guide you. Whichever format you decide to use, keep in mind that your aim is to capture your strongest qualities, focused on your new job objective. Your professional-style resume will show the interviewer and/or potential employer you are qualified for that desired position.

When you have completed your first draft, review this book's first two chapters, compare what you've written with the resumes I've included, and revise your own resume as necessary.

If your previous experiences with resume writing have proved to be more frustrating than fun, believe me, you are not alone. Perhaps under a looming job interview deadline, you tried to put something together only to have the resume turn out flat and uninviting or scattered and unfocused.

Tip: Lack of focus on your future job objective is the number one reason most resumes fail. All too often people begin a resume with the wrong focus and either are unable to complete it or else end up with an unsatisfactory product.

I have my clients at Just Resumes concentrate on *where* they are going, rather than where they have been or where they are now. In doing so, the resume makes use of your experience, of course, but in a way that amplifies and directs your skills and experiences toward your goal. By focusing on the future job objective, you can create a resume that not only points you in the right direction, but also shows the potential employer how the past and present qualify you for that job.

TIPS FOR NURSES, THERAPISTS, TECHNICIANS, AND TECHNOLOGISTS

Nurses

Tip 1   Nurses do not need to include their license number on the resume. When you go in for your interview, you will need to bring it with you. Adding this information to your resume is only using up valuable space.

Tip 2   If you are a nurse who has been in the workforce for a while but are unsure which unit you'd like to work in or you're a recent graduate of nursing school and haven't decided which area of nursing you'd like to enter, it's best to say under objective "A position in the nursing profession." This way you'll be focused in nursing, but if something special opens up you may be considered for the position. By the way, some hospitals will start nurses in specialty units right out of nursing school, but many do not. There is more about this in Chapter 5, "Resumes for the Health Care Student and Recent Graduate."

Technicians and Technologists

Tip 3   If you're a technician or technologist, you must spell it out. The job title "Lab Tech" is such a general statement that it doesn't have a meaning in the health care industry. For example, your job title would be either "Lab Technician" or "Medical Technologist."

Tip 4 The job title "Lab Assistant" or "Lab Technician" is not recognized by many hospitals. Lab Technicians are usually positions in a health care facility at a university or clinic. Hospital Lab positions are called, for example, "Phlebotomy Technician" or "Medical Technologist."

Tip 5 Whether a Medical Technologist or a Radiologist Technologist, all *registered* technologists should include their registration on the resume, as your educational background does not imply that you are registered.

Audiologists and Speech-Language Therapists

Tip 6 It is highly recommended that Audiologists (CCC-A) and Speech-Language Therapists (CCC-SP) include their certification on the resume as many practicing therapists are not certified.

TIPS FOR ALL HEALTH CARE PROFESSIONAL JOB SEEKERS

This may be hard to believe, but many job applications live or die in the first 30 seconds of the screening process. It's in that 30-second glance that the receptionist or applications examiner decides either to forward your resume to the next step or to reject it. There are, however, several strategies you can use to increase your chances of having your resume reviewed by the interviewer.

Tip 1 Keep your resume to one or two pages. You'll notice in the resume samples section of this book that almost all the resumes are one page in length. Because they are concise and to the point, the resumes clearly provide the information needed to convey your abilities and strengths. Of course if you have so much experience that one page will not suffice, do use two pages to get the job done. In any case, don't try the faulty approach of using a smaller and smaller typeface to cram all the information onto one page. You don't want to make the employer's job any tougher than it is by handing in a hard-to-read resume.

Tip 2 Your educational background always goes at the end of the resume unless you are a recent graduate and your degree is stronger than your experience or if you're applying for a job at an educational institution or factory.

Tip 3 State your objective. I advise clients to have an objective on their resumes, even a general objective. Faced with dozens of applications each day, the receptionist doing the initial screening job does not want to take the time to determine what position you're applying for at the organization or hospital. You'll also look more focused and, in turn, more desirable for the position than those whose resumes lack the objective. Their loss is your gain.

Consider this incident from Just Resumes. A woman contacted me who had had her resume done for her by another professional resume writer. She was receiving responses but for the wrong jobs. When I examined her materials, I saw that the objective was in her cover letter but not in her resume. And by reading the resume (without an objective), I could see how she appeared qualified for several types of jobs, even though she was only interested in one. We worked together, adding a job objective and rewriting the resume so that its components pointed directly to that objective. With a revised resume, now focused on her objective, she did receive a positive response from the very company she'd written to previously, but this time for the position she desired.

RESUME CHARACTERISTICS

As I mentioned earlier, there are three basic resume formats: the chronological, the functional, and the combination. The chronological style emphasizes your jobs and is written in reverse chronological order. The functional style highlights your skills with a lesser emphasis on the job titles. A combination style makes use of both the chronological and the functional strengths.

Most of you will already be familiar with the chronological format, the more traditional style. Just remember that the functional, chronological, and combination resume should offer the same information; the difference is in how the information is presented, in what is emphasized.

PERSONAL DATA

With today's equal opportunity requirements, personal data are not required, indeed do not belong, on a resume. I'll tell you a trade secret. Personnel agencies have admitted to me that they've seen examples of prejudice from the persons who screen resumes. Sometimes the screener may not even be aware of it.

SUMMARY OF RESUME STYLES

▶ The chronological format highlights the progress you've made in your jobs.

▶ The functional format highlights your skills.

▶ The combination format combines the chronological and functional formats to highlight selected jobs.

THE RESUME APPEARANCE: READY, GET SET, TYPE

The typeface you select is almost as important as the format you use for your resume. And with today's ever-expanding computer typefaces, the choices can be overwhelming. To simplify the matter, opt for something that looks professional and is easy to read. A good typeface should enhance but not dominate your overall resume presentation. (See the resume samples in Chapter 11.) Avoid the temptation to use a fancy script style; more effective are such tested stalwarts as Helvetica, Century Schoolbook or Times Roman, which are all available through laser printing and desktop publishing on both the Macintosh and IBM computer systems.

Don't scrimp when it comes to selecting your resume paper; color and texture are the important factors. For the medical profession, a brilliant white conveys a sense of competence (and perhaps hygienic cleanliness). Ivory works well for every profession. Really, whether you're a nurse, medical technologist or therapist, your personal preference plays a part in this, too.

There are many different textured papers for you to choose from. Parchment paper, for example, has a light textured background woven into the paper. Classic Laid, which also works great with resumes, has a heavier smooth woodlike finished look. Classic Linen has a lighter clothlike textured look, and cotton, the most expensive, feels and looks just like cotton.

As with the typeface you choose, the resume paper should complement your resume, *not* dominate it. Resume paper and matching envelopes are available at your local copy shop.

RESUME DO'S AND DON'TS

▶ DO choose a job that you "love."

▶ DO spend time listing all your good qualities. This is where you get credit where credit's due.

▸ DO include a job objective, clear and concise; focus your resume on your objective to show the employer how the past and present qualify you for that job.

▸ DO include experience directly related to the objective.

▸ DO start each sentence with a vigorous action word.

▸ DO list all related experience, paid or unpaid, if you're a recent graduate or are reentering the workforce. Include experience from community service, internships and/or volunteer work.

▸ DO research the position and organization before the interview.

▸ DO keep your resume down to one or two pages.

▸ DO follow up the interview with a personalized thank you letter.

▸ DON'T leave out the job objective.

▸ DON'T include material or history not related to the job objective.

▸ DON'T use long, repetitive explanations.

▸ DON'T include personal history.

▸ DON'T presume that the "personnel screener" understands skills included in the job title—tailor your job description.

▸ DON'T take for granted skills that you perform well as a matter of course.

▸ DON'T replace a job description with a job title—it's not self-explanatory. A staff nurse in one hospital may not have the same responsibilities as a staff nurse at another organization.

▸ DON'T forget to include your GPA under education, if you're a student or recent graduate and it's a 3.5 or higher.

▸ DON'T list references from whom you have not received permission or a positive response.

▸ DON'T send a "form" thank you letter. Personalize each one.

▸ DON'T BE AFRAID TO SHOW OFF YOUR SKILLS.

2

The No-Nonsense Approach to Resume Writing

In a professionally designed resume, you can convey a significant amount of information concisely and vigorously. Single-line phrases and sentences are simple to read, straightforward, and direct the employer's attention toward your capabilities and desired experiences. But again, if you prefer paragraph form, that can be quite effective, though I find one-liners are more easily noticed and understood. In either case, begin each sentence with an action word, such as "developed" or "implemented," describing what you do. (See list "More Than 100 Action Words" at the end of this chapter.)

Action words energize your resume, but avoid using the same action word twice within one job description or, if using the functional format, twice in the Experience subsection. Remember, for a functional resume, you will create subsections. The title of each subsection will depend on the skills you are highlighting as you aim toward that career objective. (See resume samples, Chapter 11.)

REMEMBER: ALWAYS THINK POSITIVE AND FOCUS THE RESUME ON YOUR JOB OBJECTIVE.

THE BASIC RESUME ELEMENTS

Whether you decide to use the chronological, functional, or combination format will depend on the way you want to present your information. Your own background and your objective will determine which resume style will work best for you. No matter what the format, however, each resume should offer the same basic information.

The resume you will create, be it functional, combination, or chronological, will incorporate these basic sections:

▸ Name, address, and phone number.

▸ Career objective.

▸ Professional profile (optional).

▸ Education and registration or certification.

▸ Description of work experience.

▸ Employment history with job title, organization name, location, and dates of employment.

Keep in mind:

▸ All sentences start with a vigorous action verb.

▸ All job descriptions and experiences focus on the career objective.

▸ Education is placed after Professional Experience, unless you are applying for health care position with an educational institution or organization or you are a recent college graduate whose education is a stronger factor than your limited work experience.

PREPARING THE CHRONOLOGICAL RESUME, STEP BY STEP

In the traditional chronological resume, you combine the experience and the employment history under one section. Each position is listed with the dates of employment, job title, organization name, city, and state, followed by a point-by-point description of job experience. Jobs are listed in reverse order beginning with the most recent position.

The chronological resume highlights the progress in your jobs. Because of this, it works best for *professionals* who are making an upward career move in the health care profession.

As an example, let's say you are a staff nurse/relief supervisor for a nursing home, and you are being considered for a position as charge nurse/supervisor for a staff of nurses at a hospital. Your previous positions, though different in nature, show a progression toward your goal: evening clinic nurse for an outpatient clinic, relief supervisor/staff nurse for a mid-size hospital, hospice nurse/acting director and trainer of entry-level employees for a larger hospital. A chronological resume, with appropriate job descriptions, would perfectly represent your career growth and development leading to this latest position.

Use the chronological resume format when all these three points apply to you:

1. Your entire employment history shows progress with skills related to your objective. (Let's say you began your career as an emergency medical technician I moved up to Emergency Medical Technician II, and then became a mobile crisis intervention specialist. Now you're aiming for director of crisis intervention unit, which follows directly from your previous experience.)

2. Each position involves a generally different job description. (Looking at the above example, each position—from technician to specialist—incorporates more responsibility and different job descriptions. The technician provides basic emergency medical services and the specialist performs more complex emergency medical decision making.)

3. Your work history is stable.

If your job history is reflected in these points and you are aiming for a position that seems to follow from what you've previously been doing, then create a chronological resume by following these instructions:

1. List your name, address, and phone number. (College students: Include your campus and permanent address, if you have one.)

2. Objective.

   What's your current objective? Make it brief and to the point. For example, "An Occupational Therapist position."

3. Profile.

   This is a brief description or summary of your skills, personality traits, and achievements related to the job objective. What are personality traits? These are your particular characteristics that demonstrate your talents and abilities on the job. This is very important to the health care profession. For example, let's say you want to be an X-ray technician. The interviewer will look for someone who is detail oriented with good communication skills.

4. Education.

   Degree (BS, MS), major, school, graduation date? If you're registered or certified, make sure to include this information here.

5. Professional experience or related experience.

What date (year starting/ending) did you start your present job? What's the organization (name, city, and state) you presently work for? Describe what you did at each job. Include any special achievements you've accomplished, related to your objective. Always focus on your strongest points, directly related to your career objective. Be consistent and repeat the preceding questions under experience for each position pertinent to your objective. Look at resume samples for more details. Remember, start with your most recent job and work backwards in *reverse* chronological order.

EXAMPLE

Pediatric Physical Therapist   1985–present
Ft. Collins Pediatric Clinic, Ft. Collins, CO

- Assess patient's personal background and medical history while gaining his/her trust and confidence.
- Perform tests and take measurements that determine a patient's strengths, weaknesses and ability to function.
- Develop appropriate treatment plan, including treatment to be provided, purpose, and anticipated outcomes and goals.
    - Goals include helping patients attain maximum functional independence, improve muscle strength and physical skills while helping them adapt to what may be permanent physical abilities.
- Work with patients to improve mobility and prevent or limit permanent disability.

For more variations on the Professional Experience theme, consult the chronological resume samples in Chapter 11.

Now, once you have created the segment for your present job, repeat the procedure for each of your previous job experiences.

PREPARING THE FUNCTIONAL RESUME, STEP BY STEP

Even with a quick glance, a functional resume looks different from a chronological resume. The functional format, because it highlights your skills, devotes a great deal more space to describing your experience. Such sections might include Management and Supervision, Hospice Home Care, Acute Emergency Assessment and Intervention to name a few. Conversely, the actual employment history will be listed at the end of the resume and will concisely give the basic information as to job title, locations, and dates.

So, in the functional resume:

▶ All the work experience is highlighted by creating subsections pertinent to the job objective.

▶ The entire employment history is listed at the end with job title, organization name, city, state, and dates of employment, each job in reverse chronological order, but without a detailed explanation of the experience.

If you are a first-time job seeker or are changing careers or reentering the job market, the functional resume works best. (Does the following information sound similar to your own background?)

1. Your entire work history goes beyond the skills and experience related to your objective.

2. You have skills related to your job objective but not necessarily in your employment history.

3. You've had several positions with the same job description.

A functional resume is designed to be selective. If your entire work history includes additional skills not related to your career objective, you'll only highlight those skills pertinent to your objective.

If you've had several positions with the same job description, you don't need to repeat yourself. You'll only say what you did one time, which saves both space on the resume for other valuable information and time for the resume examiner. Don't worry that you might be minimizing your achievements, because you will, of course, list the jobs that cover similar experience under Employment History. (See functional resume samples, Chapter 11.) As you become familiar with the functional resume, you'll see how it can convey a great deal of information in a minimum amount of space. Now, follow these instructions:

1. List your name, address, and phone number. (College students: Include your campus and permanent address, if you have one.)

2. Objective.

What is your current objective? For example, "A Director of Nursing position." Make it brief and to the point.

3. Profile.

This is optional but useful. It's this section that my clients often refer to when they say "I can't believe this is me!" or "I hadn't thought about myself before in this light!" This applies especially to those of you in the health care profession who seem a bit coy about putting all your wonderful working traits on paper. Do it. It will show the employer that you are aware of them. Your profile is a brief description or summary of working style, personality traits, and achievements that relate to your objective. These are the essence of what the employer may be looking for in the applicant; for example, "Ability to deal with sensitive situations in a highly professional and concerned manner." (See resume samples, Chapter 11.)

4. Education.

Degree (BS, MS), major, school, graduation date? If you're registered or certified, make sure to include this information here.

5. Professional experience or related experience.

Here's the heart of your functional resume. Starting with the appropriate action word, describe what you do at your job. You'll use subheads to really convey your skills. (See "More Than 100 Action Words" at the end of this chapter.) Part of the section would look like this:

PROFESSIONAL EXPERIENCE

Acute Emergency Assessment and Intervention

- Maintained superior performance in intensive care unit for eight years: general . . . medical . . . surgical . . . coronary care . . . post trauma . . . neurological.
- Served as the only evening shift nurse at a 400-bed facility.
- Responded to cardiac arrest situations throughout the hospital as an eight-year member of the Code Blue Team.
- Assisted in the Emergency Room as needed.

Hospice Home Care

- Became expert in pain control and symptom management for five years.
  - Assessed patient's pain and quickly determined best analgesic and method of delivery.

— Counseled patients and offered emotional and spiritual support to terminally ill adults and their families.

— Coordinated overall home care program with other community resources and services throughout Larimer County.

Remember to include any special achievements directly related to your career objective. Always focus on your strongest points that tie in to your career objective. For more details and examples, look at the functional resume samples in Chapter 11.

6. Employment history.

In this section, list your job title, company name, city, state, and date position started/ended in chronological order, starting with the most recent and working backward. Health care students and women returning to the workforce may not have a job title. (I'll show you what to do about that in Chapters 3 and 5.) If your job title is nondescript or if you don't have a job title, give yourself credit where credit is due. Be descriptive: when selecting an appropriate job title that best encapsulates what you do, remember that many organizations and hospitals may have a different title for what is essentially the same job. For example, you might be called a staff nurse where you work, but your job may include more managerial duties than the title implies. Another organization might call that same job staff/relief charge nurse.

ORGANIZING THE EXPERIENCE SECTION IN A FUNCTIONAL RESUME

What you do in one part of the resume can help you flesh out other sections. This is especially the case for the Professional Experience section. I suggest that you first list your Employment or Work History before becoming more specific in describing your experience. Even though this information will be listed at the bottom of your resume, you'll gain a better perspective on what you're going to write about.

What you include under the Professional Experience heading essentially will be a description of your achievements and what you've done, taken directly from the Employment or Work History section. Remember, always focus the entire experience section on your career objective.

At this stage, you can afford to be expansive. Brainstorm your ideas. There really is no limit to the categories you can create. Start with an action word describing your experiences. After you've listed your achievements and experiences directly related to your career objective, sort out what you wrote. Then, create the subtitles that fit the description of your career objective. For example, let's say you're a Regulator, Clinical Affairs Coordinator. You've probably gained valuable skills in coordinating international and domestic medical devices. These very labels can become the categories under Professional Experience that you will then expand upon.

With this procedure, you're accomplishing two things. First, you're putting in concrete form a description of the many (and often unstated) ways you work. Second, you're highlighting the skills the interviewer will be looking for in you.

So, now that you have those skills and/or areas of expertise listed as categories under Professional Experience, you can then use them as subheadings. If, as in the preceding example, you have a subheading for Regulator, Clinical Affairs Coordinator, you now add the details of what that role involves. Let's say something like:

Domestic Medical Device Regulator

- Prepare new product submittals to file with the FDA.
- Write and coordinate Investigational Device Exemptions (IDE) submissions.
- Coordinate and monitor clinical investigations.
- Develop and coordinate 510(k) submissions.
- Edit and coordinate product data sheet and literature projects.
- Provide regulatory support to product development/marketing personnel.

International Medical Device Regulator

- Coordinate communications with international distributors to ensure regulatory compliance is met. Knowledge of 1992 EEC ramifications.
- Prepare export approval requests for investigational devices.
- Introduced 56 catalog and special product devices to the Canadian market via Device Notifications and Notice of Compliance documents.
- Coordinate document translations as required by government regulations.

As you create your functional resume, visualize the employer receiving your final version. (Remember, you're aiming for that interview; keep your resume on that target; keep your achievements and experience related to your career objective.)

PREPARING THE COMBINATION RESUME, STEP BY STEP

The combination resume allows the job seeker to highlight a specific job or selected jobs and still list other work experience or employment history. It is a combination of the chronological and functional resume. For example, I designed a combination resume for a client whose objective was to work as a pharmacy technician for a large medical center. She was a pharmacist technician for another medical center where she had been employed for the past several years. Her prior experience included 5 years of pharmacy experience at retail drug stores. So, we highlighted her current employment experience at the medical center and listed her employment history of previous retail drug store locations in the combination resume style. This format works great for those with the following background:

1. You've had specific job(s) directly related to your objective.
2. Each position involves a completely different job description.
3. And, you also have related jobs that are important to mention because they are indirectly related to your current objective.
4. If you're a student, Items 1 and 2 apply to your background, and you have jobs you'd like to mention just to show your stable work history.

For some of you, certain jobs you've had deserve more emphasis than others. A combination resume brings attention to the jobs most directly related to your career objective. A variation on the chronological and functional formats, the combination resume highlights the jobs that tie in to your objective by using the chronological style. Then it lists your other employment in the functional format. The combination format has an extensive job description for a specific job or jobs and then includes in a different section a job listing of your previous employment history.

To create a combination resume, begin by following the same instructions for the chronological resume but this time you'll highlight selected job(s) under the professional experience section that relate directly to your job objective. (See instructions 1–5, in the section "Preparing the Chronological Resume.") In addition, you will also create a section for your previous jobs, titled Employment History, and list them at the end of your resume. List your job title, organization name, city, state, and date position started and ended for the rest of your jobs in chronological order, starting with the most recent and working backward as in the functional resume. (See resume samples in Chapter 11.)

> *NOTE:* IF YOU'VE HAD NUMEROUS JOBS OVER THE YEARS, YOU DON'T *HAVE* TO LIST THEM ALL.

OPTIONAL RESUME HEADINGS

All resumes incorporate some flexibility. You may list the following skills or activities under the Professional Profile section or create titles for anything that's pertinent to your career objective and is important to you, such as:

Special Training	Affiliations
Office Skills	Special Skills
Publications	Computer Skills
Volunteer Work	Other Pertinent Information
Academic Achievements	Language Skills

MORE THAN 100 ACTION WORDS

act as	contribute	enact
active in	control	establish
administer	coordinate	evaluate
allocate	correct	edit
analyze	correspond	execute
approve	counsel	examine
articulate	create	follow-up
assimilate	coach	forecast
assist	chair	formulate
assure	demonstrate	forward
augment	design	generate
balance	determine	guided
built	develop	identify
collect	direct	implement
communicate	distribute	improve
compute	document	initiate
conceptualize	draft	integrate
consolidate	delegate	interface
consult	effect	install

institute	prepare	refer
interview	present	schedule
instruct	produce	screen
launch	proofread	secure
liaison	promote	process
locate	propose	select
lecture	provide	set up
lead	perform	supervise
maintain	persuade	supply
manage	recommend	specify
monitor	repair	systematize
mediate	recruit	stimulate
market	report	summarize
optimize	research	strengthen
organize	resolve	test
oversee	review	train
operate	revise	tabulate
plan	represent	upgrade

3

Health Care Professionals Returning to the Workforce

Those of you who have been removed from the workforce for many years may be concerned that you've been out of the cycle too long to plug back in. It is true, in most hospitals and organizations, if you're a nurse and you have been out of the workforce for more than five years, you have been out of the job market for a long time because of the forever changing trends in the health care industry. What should you do?

Tip: While some hospitals and organizations will hire a nurse who has been out of the workforce for many years, most will require you to take a refresher course. The refresher course is available at hospitals through on-the-job training and special programs as well as at community colleges throughout the nation.

The refresher course usually offers didactic and clinical portions focusing on the more recent trends in health care. For example, you'll learn about the universal barrier, a newer technique used for preventing the spread of any virus.

Subjects covered are pharmacology and law and ethics with emphasis on different areas of nursing, such as medical-surgical nursing including units of fluid electrolytes; acid-base balance; concepts of homeostasis; circulatory system; pulmonary system; and renal system. Other important concepts cover documentation, which has changed dramatically, becoming much more detailed.

Tip: Medical technology is progressing rapidly. Medical technologists who have been out of the job market for a while should be prepared to do their homework and seek an organization that offers on-the-job training.

On the other hand, in some health care professions, such as the medical social worker, those who have been out of the workforce for many years will be able to focus on other skills they may have demonstrated during the intervening years.

Tip: If you're a medical social worker returning to the workforce, and you possess excellent people skills, many social worker supervisors feel you have the ability to learn the rest, such as new forms of paperwork and technical skills for the job.

For example, if you are a housewife/mom: Remember to include in your resume the committees you've served on, the school projects you've dived into, the volunteer work you've done—these are all valuable sources of material for your resume.

Or consider a sick or disabled family member(s) or friend(s) you've been involved with for several years. Yes, it's a voluntary, unpaid position, but take a few minutes to analyze what you've done, and suddenly you'll be coming up with a variety of useful skills. Write down the kinds of activities you've been engaged in for the friend you helped nurse back to good health. Maybe you brought in a speaker or attended meetings to support a friend through the 12-step program. Whatever your experience, once you've generated a list, create two or three subsections, such as:

Organization Skills

Interpersonal Communication Skills

Counseling-Related Skills

Advocate Skills

One of the beauties of a functional resume is that you can give yourself credit for the experience you've gained and for the skills you've developed during your years away from the work world as well, even if you never received a single paycheck for what you did.

Place each experience under the appropriate heading. As you do this, picture the employer who is going to read your resume. What will that person be looking for? Like the other resumes in this book, your resume will include a career objective; emphasize those achievements and experiences that are related to your objective.

You might be amazed at the significant experiences you can come up with. Even day-to-day activities can suddenly appear in a different light if you take a step back and process exactly what you do. Under the category of family–time management you have probably been scheduling appointments and travel arrangements for your children and husband, chauffeuring your offspring to school and afternoon activities, while still managing to have dinner on the table at 6:30 P.M.. Listen, you know something about deadlines and organization!

Have you ever rushed a family member off to the emergency room or nursed someone through a long illness or personal crisis? Those kinds of actions require strong interpersonal communication skills and the ability to deal with high-pressure situations calmly, quickly, and efficiently.

You can use "hidden" skills such as these to your advantage in a functional resume. It is just a matter of placing those skills under the appropriate subtitle. For example:

Interpersonal Communication   Communication
People Management   Organization
Problem Solving   Finance
Time Management

If you actually have work experience but haven't been employed in many years, the functional resume also works well in this situation. First, you will be highlighting your skills under Related Experience. Then, you will be listing your work history at the bottom of the resume. (See resume samples in Chapter 11).

But how will you fill the gap in time when you weren't in a paid job? Simple, you'll say something like this:

Home Management, Study, Research, Madison, WI, 1985–present

or

Home Management, Travel, Studies, Ft. Collins, CO, 1975–92

Not only does this arrangement fill any gaps in your resume, it also explains what you've been doing, where, and when. Plus, it also proves to you that you have been accomplishing something of significance.

Here's another typical (and often overlooked) example. A client came to me for help and said, "I'd like to be a doctor's assistant, but I don't have any experience; I've been helping out my husband in his office and have spent the rest of my time being a mom and housewife." Well, in putting together the resume, we discovered plenty of experience that any doctor's office would look for in her. By the way, her husband is a doctor.

4

Changing Careers or Moving up in the Health Care Profession

The health care profession is a fast-growing and ever-demanding field. Once you get your degree and/or license there is a great demand for health care professionals. Not only are there shortages of some positions, there are also new positions opening up every year. You might be in the health assessment and treatment occupation, health diagnosis, health service, health technologist or technician, or other area, and at some point, whether by necessity or choice, you want to either advance to a higher position or move sideways into a related field. Regardless of the business climate—whether we're in the midst of a recession or a booming economy—an effective resume can help you reposition yourself.

You need a way of clearly showing your progress and achievements, highlighted in a resume that will not only be competitive but will get results. You want to show your potential employers that you are thinking in terms of a career and not just a job.

If you feel you are not advancing as quickly as you think you deserve to, a professional resume emphasizing your work history can offer you the psychological boost you need to present yourself in the best possible light. Not only will your resume show them your capabilities, it will also show *you* what you have done, allowing you to see yourself in a positive and focused manner aiming toward that goal.

MOVING UP

The best format for charting your experience if you are moving up is with the chronological format. As I showed in Chapter 2, the chronological resume details your progress most clearly by highlighting your employment history.

MAKING A LATERAL MOVE

If you are making a lateral move to another organization or department but essentially staying in the health care field, use the functional style, which will emphasize your job skills. (Refer to Chapter 2 for directions to create your resume.)

In all cases, remember to focus on your career objective. Highlight all the training you have received and the duties you're currently responsible for.

In the past, employees tended to stay with one employer for longer periods of time, even for whole careers. People also remained in the same field for the most part. But these days, it is not at all unusual for many of us to begin in our twenties in one field, move over to another area of work in our thirties, and again switch gears in our forties. A former dietitian or nutritionist may take up a health educator position or become a home economist or food service manager. A medical assistant may become a dental assistant, or an occupational or physical therapist aide. An emergency medical technician may become a registered nurse, police officer, or fire fighter.

This fluidity of professional development calls for the functional resume, because you are going to be focusing on your skills, not just your employment history. You may be a therapist aiming for a change as a nurse, and embedded in your past are skills and strengths that apply to that new career objective. Using the functional resume will give you more options when deciding what to highlight.

For example, let's say you are currently a social service aide and a former preschool teacher's aide. Over the past five years, you worked closely with a disabled child. Excited by watching the progress of the child through that experience, you decided you'd like to become a pediatric physical therapist and recently received your license. Now, how do you best present yourself? Using a functional resume format, you'll create the heading of Related Experience. For example:

Physical Therapy Assistant
- Assisted therapist in classroom with special equipment and exercise to improve strength, endurance, and coordination of a child

from birth to three years of age diagnosed with Athetoid Distonic Cerebral Palsy.

- Worked with therapist to help patient maximize performance of day-to-day activities and instruct parent's therapies to do at home.
- Therapy resulted in the patient able to hold head up and sit up by the age of 18 months and stand while holding furniture by the age of two and a half.

Social Service Aide/Organization Skills

- Worked with developmentally disabled in community preparation program.
- Taught socialization skills to older men and women for community living.
- Assisted in directing a play-therapy program involving multiply handicapped children and their foster grandparents.

What can often lead to a career change is the discovery about yourself that you make when you pursue a new hobby, take a class, or, as in the case above, help a friend or family member on a special project. These are more than "hidden" skills; they are true indicators of your interest that translate so well into the essence of a functional resume.

5

Resumes for the Health Care Student and Recent Graduate

You can study hard in school for four years, graduate with honors, and yet when it comes time to enter the job market, the interviewer's first request is "to see a copy of your resume."

A good resume—one that represents your hard-earned skills and accomplishments—will help you bridge the gap between college and the work world.

Some college graduates are frustrated because they feel they don't have enough previous employment to allow them to find a decent job. They hear so much about the importance of practical experience. Others may believe that they're good prospects, but they fear their grade point average may keep them from being considered by the organizations they really want to work for. GPA requirements do not apply to health care professionals in many of the hospitals. They look for a lot more than transcripts, such as: Are you people oriented? Can you act quickly and calmly in a highly stressful emergency situation?

Some hospitals will start a recent graduate or student nurse in the medical-surgical units and not in specialty areas, whereas other hospitals will start the recent graduate in a specialty unit with an orientation. Do your homework, call around to several organizations and get information. Find out what each one does have to offer.

Tip: Paid summer internships, not affiliated with the college, are available the summer before graduation at hospitals nationwide. This is the time for showing how valuable you are to the organization.

For the majority of college students, a functional resume highlighting skills is the ticket to getting that interview. Most college students do not have enough experience to warrant using a chronological resume. However, a student who has had several unrelated paid jobs and has also had internships and/or volunteer committee or other work experience can list those unpaid though valuable assets under Experience in the flexible combination resume.

STUDENTS, GRADUATES, AND THE TWO-PAGE RESUME

As in the case of most professional resume writers, students and recent graduates usually should be able to create a one-page resume. Some graduates, however, may have an abundance of related experience requiring a two-page resume. That is all right. I would rather you have a well-written and properly formatted two-page resume than a poorly written, crowded one-pager. Don't use a smaller typeface in hopes of getting all the information onto one page. Such a tactic will hinder rather than improve your job chances. No employer wants to bother with a hard-to-read resume.

Here are a couple of pointers for those of you with a two-page resume. Add the notation "-More-" or "-Continued-" at the bottom of the first page. Place your name and the words "page two" at the top of the second page.

COLLEGE GRADUATES ENTERING THE PROFESSIONAL WORLD

Some college graduates have previous paid experience involving skills that directly relate to the jobs they're applying for. For example, during your junior and senior college years let's say you had a part-time job as a physician assistant for a private practice, and now, as a graduate, you are seeking a position with a hospital in another city. You would use the chronological format to detail your job experiences that point you in the direction of your future position. The chronological resume format works best in this situation because it emphasizes the jobs you have held that directly lead toward your career objective.

WHAT IF YOU HAVE NO PAID EXPERIENCE?

Many college students do not have any paid job experience that ties into their job objective. That might seem to be an insurmountable barrier, for as we all know, many organizations won't hire someone until he or she has experience in the field. But how do you obtain experience if no one will hire you?

Well, don't give up. I've found that most of my clients, even students, have some sort of related experience to write about in their resume for that upcoming job or they wouldn't be interested in applying for it.

Think back over your school years. Perhaps you worked on school projects related to your job objective. Or what about those committees you've been an active member of. And don't forget volunteer work and/or internships in your field. Also include any special achievements that are directly related to your career objective.

In a functional style, here's how I would arrange the resume for a second-year student with school project experience who wants to find part-time work in a clinical lab.

Under Education we would list related classes taken, and under Related Experience we would create the appropriate subheading as shown below:

Under Objective: A *Clinical Lab Assistant* internship.

Under Education: *BS Degree, Medical Technology,* 1993
University of Nebraska, Lincoln, NE

Related Courses: Chemistry, Biological Science, Microbiology, Mathematics, Lab Clinic

Under Related Experience:

Chemical Lab Test Projects
- Perform chemical tests to determine blood glucose or cholesterol levels.
- Examine tissue to detect the presence of infections or diseases.
- Use highly sophisticated computerized instruments to perform these tests.

Microscopic Lab Test Projects
- Examine blood, tissue, and other body substances.
- Make cultures of body fluid or tissue samples to determine the presence of bacteria, fungi, parasites, or other microorganisms.
- Analyze samples for chemical content or reaction.

You certainly don't have to be a medical technology student to apply this method to your situation. Pharmacology majors who have been interns, nursing students who practiced internships at the university hospital—all of you can demonstrate to your potential employers that you do have the experience to move into paid employment.

For those of you with internship experience and unrelated previous employment (fast foods, sales clerk, etc.), I recommend the combination resume format, which I discussed in Chapter 2. Basically, you will highlight your internship or selected job(s) as in a chronological format under the Related Experience heading and place your other jobs under Employment History at the bottom of the resume as in the functional format.

This method helps to solve the Catch-22 problem in which an organization won't hire you unless you have experience and it seems impossible to gain experience unless you get hired. By pinpointing your projects and volunteer work, you can demonstrate to employers and to yourself that you do have what it takes to obtain that valued first job.

THE FIRST-YEAR STUDENT VERSUS THE RECENT COLLEGE GRADUATE

Most of you soon-to-be graduates are seeking *full-time* work. But what if you're a first- or second-year student seeking *part-time* employment or an internship in your field of study? Go for it! The key word here is *part-time*. To some employers, a first-year student means stability. Employers feel there's a good chance students will plan on staying with the organization throughout their school years. That could mean 2 to 4 years of employment for you.

6

The Cover Letter and Thank You Letter

ABOUT COVER LETTERS

Most resumes are not complete without a cover letter, which introduces you and your resume to the employer. Providing essential information not found in the resume, cover letters are needed whenever you mail your resume to an employer. They can be personalized or generalized but are written specifically to go with the individual's resume. You can create an effective cover letter in three paragraphs.

1. The first paragraph states why you are writing it, that is, what position you're applying for and whether you saw an advertisement or heard about the position or company through a referral or by reputation.

2. The second paragraph is a brief summary stating why you feel qualified for the position. What makes you different? If adding the Professional Profile section in a resume will make an otherwise one-page resume into two pages, I'll use it in a cover letter instead. Never use it for both or repeat verbatim what is said in the resume.

3. The third paragraph is the closing statement saying where you can be reached and thanking the employer. See the following cover letter sample.

SAMPLE COVER LETTER

August 12, 1992

Rachel Weiss, Personnel Director
Poudre Valley Hospital
1234 Robertson Way
Ft. Collins, CO 80524

Dear Rachel Weiss:

I am writing in response to your advertisement in *The Coloradoan,* dated August 12, 1992, for the position of Staff Nurse.

I have recently received my nursing license after completing a summer internship at Poudre Valley Hospital. My dedication and enthusiasm for nursing extends far beyond the call of duty. I am on several committees that promote the health and wellness of the community. I am confident I will make a significant contribution to your hospital staff now, and an increasingly important one in years to come.

Enclosed is my resume for your review. I am available at the address and phone number above at your earliest convenience. Thank you for your time and consideration.

Sincerely,

Katlyn O'Brien

ABOUT THANK YOU LETTERS

A thank you letter is sent after you've had an interview for a position you're interested in. The thank you letter should be mailed the day of the interview; it should be brief and personalized. Follow this three-paragraph procedure:

1. In the opening paragraph thank the interviewer, reemphasizing your interest in the position.
2. The second paragraph reminds the employer why you are a good candidate for the position. Mention something specific from the interview.
3. The closing paragraph again adds a thanks and states that you look forward to hearing from the interviewer.

Sending a thank you letter after the interview will reinforce in the interviewer's mind just how serious and enthusiastic you are about the position. That very act can separate you from the other applicants, giving you the extra something that leads to your being hired.

SAMPLE THANK YOU LETTER

August 16, 1992

Dear Mrs. Cowley:

Thank you for spending so much time with me yesterday. I am very excited about the prospect of attaining a staff nursing position with Poudre Valley Hospital.

I'm happy to say, we share the same philosophy in what it takes to offer quality health care. Being aware of your Mission Statement along with your excellent reputation and commitment to the health care industry, I would be proud to be a member of your nursing staff.

If you have any questions, feel free to call me at any time.

Sincerely,

Daphney Johnson

7

Job Trends to Look for in the Health Care Industry

JOB TRENDS FOR THE 1990s: WHAT DIRECTION IS THE HEALTH CARE INDUSTRY GOING?

According to the U.S. Department of Labor Bureau of Labor Statistics Occupational Outlook Handbook, the health care industry will continue to be one of the most important groups of industries in the economy in terms of job creation. Employment in the health services industry is projected to grow in 1991 from 8.2 to 11.3 million by the year 2000.

Fact: The federal government is currently working on the Clinical Laboratory Improvement Act (CLIA), which is expected to be in effect by 1992.

The CLIA is an act to regulate all clinical laboratories—including private physician office laboratories—on ethics, quality, and precision. This will involve regulation on the types of testing being done and the personnel being hired. It will require medical technologists to do all the testing, instead of nurses. The personnel they hire will be required to pass a controlled proficiency test for every test done.

New technology and growing and aging population will increase the demand for health services. Because of the rapid expansion of health care employment, 7 of the 10 fastest growing occupations between 1988 and 2000 will be health related. Not all the health industries will grow at the same rate; outpatient care facilities and offices of "other health practitioners," including chiropractors, optometrists, psychologists, and other practitioners will be increasing the fastest.

Hospitals, both private and public, will be growing more slowly than all the other health industries, but faster than the average for all industries. Nonetheless, hospitals will continue to employ the most workers among the health care industries.

The job listings and occupation descriptions in this chapter are taken from the U.S. Department of Labor Bureau of Labor Statistics, Occupational Outlook Handbook, 1990–1991 Edition. This valuable information, along with the resume samples in Chapter 11, can help you describe job experiences in your own resume. Whether you are moving up; making a lateral change; deciding, as a college student, which direction to go; or entering the professional world, as a recent graduate, this chapter will be instrumental in helping you to make the right decision for your future.

JOB TITLES OF KEY HEALTH CARE PROFESSIONS

Health Service Occupations

Dental Assistants	Occupational Therapy Assistants
Medical Assistants	Physical Therapy Assistants
Nursing Aides	Psychiatric Aides

Health Assessment and Treating Occupations

Dietitians and Nutritionists	Recreational Therapists
Clinical Dietitians	Registered Nurses
Community Dietitians	OB-GYN Nurses
Management Dietitians	Occupational Health Nurse
Research Dietitians	Utilization Review Nurse
Occupational Therapists	Nursing Director
Pharmacists	Respiratory Therapists
Physical Therapists	Speech-Language Pathologists
Physician Assistants	Audiologists

Health Technologists and Technicians

Clinical Laboratory Technologists and Technicians
Dental Hygienists
Dispensing Opticians
EEG Technologists
EKG Technicians

Emergency Medical Technicians
Licensed Practical Nurses
Medical Record Technicians
Nuclear Medicine Technologists
Radiologic Technologists
Surgical Technologists

Health Diagnosing Occupations

Chiropractors
Dentists
Optometrists

Physicians
Podiatrists
Veterinarians

JOB DESCRIPTIONS TO KEY HEALTH ASSESSMENT AND TREATING OCCUPATIONS

Dietitians and Nutritionists

Dietitians and nutritionists use their knowledge of the principles of nutrition to help people develop healthy eating habits. They are professionally trained in the science of nutrition to evaluate an individual's diet. They may suggest modifications such as instructing a client with high blood pressure to avoid salty foods, for example, or help an overweight person identify sources of fats and sugars.

Dietitians also counsel groups; set up and supervise food service systems for institutions such as hospitals, prisons and schools; and promote sound eating habits through education and research. Major areas of practice are clinical, community, and management dietetics. Dietitians also work as educators, researchers, and private practitioners.

Clinical dietitians provide nutritional service for patients in hospitals, nursing homes, clinics, or doctors' offices. They assess patients' nutritional needs, develop and implement nutrition programs, and evaluate and report the results. Clinical dietitians confer with doctors and other health care professionals about each patient in order to coordinate nutritional intake with other treatments—medications in particular. These dietitians are sometimes called therapeutic dietitians, a term that identifies them as being chiefly concerned with treating the sick.

Community dietitians counsel individuals and groups on nutritional practices designed to prevent disease and to promote good health. They are employed in such places as public health clinics, home health agencies, health maintenance organizations, and human service agencies that provide group and home-delivered meals. Their job is to evaluate individual needs, establish nutritional care plans, and communicate the principles of good nutrition in a way individuals and their families can understand. Practice opportunities for clinical and community dietitians are becoming more diverse due to increased public interest in nutrition and fitness.

Management dietitians are responsible for large-scale meal planning and preparation in such places as hospitals, nursing homes, company cafeterias, prisons, elementary and secondary schools, and colleges and universities. They supervise the planning, preparation, and service of meals; select, train, and direct other dietitians and food service supervisors and workers; budget for and purchase food, equipment, and supplies; enforce sanitary and safety regulations; and prepare records and reports.

Research dietitians are usually employed in academic medical centers or educational institutions, although some work in community health programs. Using established research methods and analytical techniques, they conduct studies in areas that range from basic science to practical applications.

Dietitians and nutritionists held about 40,000 jobs in 1988, hospitals and nursing homes being the major source of employment in this field. Employment of dietitians is expected to grow faster than the average for all occupations through the year 2000 to meet the demand for meals and nutritional counseling in settings as diverse as hospitals, schools, prisons, and health clubs.

Occupational Therapists

Occupational therapists help mentally, physically, developmentally, or emotionally disabled individuals develop, recover, or maintain daily living and work skills. They help patients improve their basic motor functions and reasoning abilities, as well as help them learn to dress, bathe, cook, or operate machinery. Occupational therapists also help permanently disabled patients cope with the physical and emotional effects of being disabled. With support and direction, patients learn (or relearn) many of the day-to-day skills necessary to establish an independent, productive, and satisfying lifestyle. Keeping notes is an important part of an occupational therapist's job. Records are always kept for purposes of evaluating the patient, reporting to the physician, and billing. Occupational therapists tend to work with individuals in a particular age group or with particular disabilities. In home health care, for instance, referrals often involve elderly patients; in schools, young children. A growing number of therapists work in the wellness and health promotion areas.

Occupational therapists held about 33,000 jobs in 1988. The largest numbers of jobs were in hospitals. School systems are the second largest employer of occupational therapists. Other major employers include nursing homes, community mental health centers, adult day-care programs, outpatient clinics, and residential care facilities. Employment of occupational therapists is expected to increase much faster than the average for all occupations through the year 2000, due to anticipated growth in demand for rehabilitation and long-term care services.

Pharmacists

Pharmacists advise the public on the proper selection and use of medicines. They also advise physicians and other health professionals. The special knowledge of the pharmacists is needed because of the complexity and potential side effects of the large and growing number of pharmaceutical products on the market.

In addition to providing information, pharmacists dispense drugs and medicines prescribed by health practitioners, such as physicians, podiatrists, and dentists. Pharmacists must understand the use, composition, and effects of drugs and how they are tested for purity and strength. Compounding—the actual mixing of ingredients to form powders, tablets, capsules, ointments, and solutions—is now only a small part of a pharmacist's practices, because most medicines are produced by pharmaceutical companies in the dosage and form used by the patient.

Pharmacists held about 162,000 jobs in 1988. The majority of pharmacists practice in community pharmacies and hospitals. Employment of pharmacists is expected to grow very rapidly due to the increased pharmaceutical needs of a larger and older population.

Physical Therapists

Physical therapists work to improve the mobility, relieve the pain, and prevent or limit the permanent disability of patients suffering from injuries or disease. Their patients include accident victims or handicapped individuals with such conditions as multiple sclerosis, cerebral palsy, nerve injuries, amputations, head injuries, fractures, low back pain, arthritis, and heart disease. Patients range in age from the newborn to the elderly. The goals include helping patients attain maximum functional independence, improved muscle strength, and physical skills while helping them adapt to what may be permanent changes in their physical abilities.

Physical therapists evaluate the patient by performing tests and taking measurements that determine a patient's strengths, weaknesses, and ability to function. Each evaluation, and the time required to conduct one, depends on the nature of the injury or impairment. For instance, football players with knee injuries usually require considerably less time than automobile accident victims with broken bones and head injuries.

Physical therapists held about 68,000 jobs in 1988. Hospitals are the largest employer; many other jobs are in private clinics, physicians' offices, home health agencies, nursing homes, outpatient care facilities, residential facilities for handicapped children, school systems, and health maintenance organizations.

Physician Assistants

Physician assistants work under the supervision of a licensed physician to take medical histories, perform physical examinations, order laboratory tests, make preliminary diagnoses, prescribe appropriate treatments and recommend medications and drug therapies. In a growing number of states, physician assistants prescribe certain medications. They also treat minor problems such as lacerations, abrasions, and burns. Some physician assistants provide pre-and postoperative care and work as first or second assistants during major surgery.

Physician assistants held about 48,000 jobs in 1988. PAs most commonly work in office-based medical practices; others work in hospitals, health maintenance organizations, public health clinics, and institutions. Employment opportunities are very good through the year 2000 due to anticipated expansion of the health service industry.

Recreational Therapists

Recreational therapy is a relatively new field. Recreational therapists, also known as therapeutic recreation specialists, employ activities to treat mentally, physically, or emotionally disabled individuals. By using various activities as a form of goal-directed treatment, therapists attempt to minimize symptoms and improve the physical, mental, and emotional well-being of their patients. Closely related to occupational therapy, it also recognizes the importance of ordinary activities in putting disabled persons on the road to improvement or full recovery. Toward this end, therapists use such activities as athletic events, dances, arts and crafts, musical activities, movies, and field trips. Recreational therapy goals include helping patients improve their physical strength and coordination, building confidence and self-esteem through assertiveness training, managing stress through relaxing activities, and learning how to express feelings in positive and effective ways.

Recreational therapists held about 26,000 jobs in 1988. Nursing homes and hospitals each employed more than one third of that number. Other employers include community mental health centers, adult day-care programs, correctional facilities, and residential facilities. Job prospects are expected to be favorable through the year 2000, especially for those with a strong clinical background who have also graduated from an accredited program.

Registered Nurses

Registered nurses (RNs) care for the sick and help people stay well. Typically concerned with the "whole person," registered nurses provide for the physical, mental, and emotional needs of their patients. They observe, assess, and record symptoms, reactions, and progress; administer medications; assist in convalescence and rehabilitation; instruct patients and their families in proper care; and help individuals and groups take steps to improve or maintain their health. While state laws govern the tasks RNs are allowed to perform, it is usually the work setting—together with the nurse's educational preparation and experience—that determines day-to-day job duties.

Hospital nurses constitute the largest group of nurses. Most are staff nurses, who provide bedside nursing care and carry out the medical regimen prescribed by physicians. They may also supervise licensed practical nurses, aides, and orderlies. Hospital nurses usually work with groups of patients who require the same type of care, for instance, those recovering from surgery, acutely ill children, trauma victims, or cancer patients.

Nursing home nurses manage nursing care for residents with conditions ranging from a fracture to Alzheimer's disease. Although they generally spend most of their time on administrative and supervisory tasks, RNs also assess residents' needs, develop treatment plans, supervise licensed practical nurses and nursing aides, and perform complex treatments such as starting intravenous fluids.

Public health nurses care for patients in clinics, schools, retirement and life care communities, and other community settings. They instruct community groups in proper nutrition and exercise and arrange for immunizations, blood pressure testing, and other health screening measures. These nurses work with community leaders, teachers, parents, and physicians in community health education.

Some public health nurses work in schools. A growing number provide, oversee, or manage home health care, where they instruct patients and families in the home and provide periodic services prescribed by a physician.

Private duty nurses provide nursing services to patients needing constant attention. They either work directly for a family or on a contract to patients. They may alternate between work in a home, hospital, nursing home, or rehabilitation center.

Office nurses assist physicians in private practice, clinics, and health maintenance organizations. Some perform routine laboratory and office work in addition to nursing duties.

Occupational health or industrial nurses provide nursing care to employees in industry and government. They treat minor injuries and illnesses at work, provide emergency care, arrange for further care if necessary, and offer health counseling. They also may assist with health examinations and inoculations.

Registered nurses held about 1,577,000 jobs in 1988. Job prospects in nursing should be excellent for quite some time. Employment is expected to grow much faster than the average for all occupations through the year 2000. This is due to the technological advances in patient care, which involve a greater number of increasingly complex services and a growing and aging population.

Respiratory Therapists

Respiratory therapists, also known as respiratory care practitioners, specialize in the evaluation, treatment, and care of patients with breathing disorders. Whenever the breath of life is at risk, the respiratory therapist is called on to intervene. Most respiratory therapists work with hospital patients in three distinct phases of care: diagnosis, treatment, and patient management. Providing respiratory care at home is a rapidly expanding area of practice. Respiratory therapists have long administered oxygen to patients in their homes. Respiratory care is also moving into new areas. A growing number of respiratory therapists are being trained to assist in the specialized treatment and rehabilitation of cardiopulmonary patients. Others are acquiring additional skills in order to specialize in respiratory care for newborn and premature infants.

Respiratory therapists held approximately 56,000 jobs in 1988. About 9 out of 10 of these jobs were in hospitals in the department of respiratory care, anesthesiology, or pulmonary medicine. Other employers include medical equipment rental companies, home health agencies, and nursing homes. Employment is expected to increase rapidly through the year 2000.

Speech-Language Pathologists

Speech-language pathologists identify and treat speech, language, and swallowing disorders resulting from conditions such as total or partial hearing loss, brain injury, cerebral palsy, cleft palate, voice pathology, mental retardation, faulty learning, emotional problems, or foreign dialect. They also counsel patients and families about communication disorders and how to cope with the stress and misunderstanding that often accompany a communication disorder. Counseling may involve little more than reassuring the client that the problem is not unique, or it may involve working with the entire family to recognize and change behavior patterns that impede communication and treatment.

Audiologists

Audiologists identify, assess, treat, and work to prevent hearing problems. In one of the basic tests, audiologists use an audiometer to measure the loudness at which sound at various frequencies becomes audible to the patient. After instructing the individual being tested to signal whenever a sound is heard, the audiologist adjusts the audiometer to emit sounds at various intensities and pitch levels. The results are assessed and then used to render a diagnosis and determine a course of treatment. This may include the fitting of a hearing aid, providing instruction in speech reading, or recommending the use of telephone and television amplifiers.

Speech-language pathologists and audiologists held about 53,000 jobs in 1988. Job outlook is greater than average for all occupations through the year 2000 because of the rapid growth in the population. Demand is expected to rise in speech and hearing clinics, physicians' offices, outpatient care facilities, nursing homes, home health agencies, and educational institutions.

JOB DESCRIPTIONS TO KEY HEALTH CARE SERVICE POSITIONS

Dental Assistants

Dental assistants work at chairside to assist dentists, and also perform laboratory and sometimes clerical work depending on the size of the practice. The assistant makes the patient as comfortable as possible in the dental chair, prepares him or her for treatment and obtains dental records. In small single-dentist practices, dental assistants may manage the office in addition to their clinical responsibilities, arranging and confirming appointments, receiving patients, keeping treatment records, sending bills, receiving payments, and ordering dental supplies and materials. Those with lab duties may, for example, make casts of the teeth and mouth from impressions taken by the dentist.

Dental assistants held about 166,000 jobs in 1988. Most dental assistants work in private dental offices. Others work in dental schools, hospital dental departments, state and local public health departments, or private clinics. Job opportunities are expected to be excellent for persons interested in entering this occupation.

Medical Assistants

Medical assistants help physicians examine and treat patients, as well as perform routine tasks needed to keep the office running smoothly.

Back Office Medical Assistants. Clinical duties vary according to state law and commonly include taking and recording vital signs and medical histories; explaining treatment procedures to patients; preparing patients for examination; and assisting during the examination. Afterward, medical assistants collect and prepare laboratory specimens or perform basic laboratory tests on the premises; dispose of contaminated supplies; and sterilize medical instruments. Other clinical duties include instructing patients about medication and special diets, authorizing drug refills as directed, telephoning prescriptions to the pharmacy, drawing blood, preparing patients for X rays, taking EKGs, and applying dressings.

Front Office Medical Assistants. Administrative duties may include answering the telephone, greeting patients, recording and filing patient medical records, filling out insurance forms, handling correspondence, scheduling appointments, arranging for hospital admission and laboratory services, handling billing, and preparing bookkeeping.

Medical assistants held approximately 149,000 jobs in 1988. Most were employed in physicians' offices. Others worked for optometrists, podiatrists, chiropractors, and hospitals. The employment growth outlook is excellent through the year 2000 due to the increased medical needs of an aging population.

Nursing Aides

Nursing aides care for physically or mentally ill, injured, disabled, or infirm individuals confined to hospitals, long-term care facilities such as nursing homes, and mental health settings. They are sometimes known as nursing assistants or hospital attendants, and work under the supervision of registered and licensed practical nurses. Typical duties include answering patients' call bells; delivering messages; serving meals; making beds; and feeding, dressing, and bathing patients. Aides may also give massages; take temperatures, pulse, respiration, and blood pressure; and assist patients in getting in and out of bed and walking.

Nursing aides held approximately 1,184,000 jobs at nursing homes, hospitals, and county mental institutions in 1988. Job prospects for this profession are expected to be excellent through the year 2000 due to the growing number of our aging population.

Psychiatric Aides

Psychiatric aides, also known as mental health assistants, psychiatric nursing assistants, or ward attendants, care for mentally impaired or emotionally disturbed individuals. They work under a team that may include psychiatrists, psychologists, psychiatric nurses, social workers, and therapists. In addition to helping patients dress, bathe, groom, and eat, psychiatric aides socialize with patients. Psychiatric aides may play games such as cards with the patients, watch television with them, or participate in group activities that are designed to elicit behavior changes. They observe patients and report any signs or actions that might be important for the professional staff to know. If necessary, they help to restrain unruly patients. Because they have the closest contact with patients, psychiatric aides have a great deal of influence on patients' outlook and treatment.

Psychiatric aides held about 114,000 jobs in 1988. Most worked in psychiatric hospitals, state and county mental institutions, or private psychiatric facilities. Employment opportunities are expected to increase rapidly through the year 2000.

JOB DESCRIPTIONS TO KEY HEALTH TECHNOLOGISTS AND TECHNICIANS POSITIONS

Clinical Laboratory Technologists and Technicians

Because changes in body fluids, tissues, and cells are often a sign that something is wrong, clinical laboratory testing plays a crucial role in the detection, diagnosis, and treatment of disease. Some clinical laboratory workers run routine tests, while others perform complex analyses. The term "technologist" is generally used for workers who are registered or certified and "technician" for those who are not.

Medical technologists perform complicated chemical, biological, hematological, immunologic, microscopic, and bacteriological tests. These may include chemical tests to determine blood glucose or cholesterol levels, for example, or examinations of tissue to detect the presence of infections or diseases. Technologists microscopically examine blood, tissue, and other body substances; make cultures of body fluid or tissue samples to determine the presence of bacteria, fungi, parasites, or other microorganisms; and analyze samples for chemical content or reaction. They also type and cross-match blood samples for transfusions.

Medical laboratory technicians perform a wide range of routine tests and laboratory procedures. Technicians may prepare specimens and operate automatic analyzers, for example, or they may perform manual tests following detailed instructions. Like technologists, they may work in several different areas of the clinical laboratory or specialize in just one.

Clinical laboratory technologists and technicians held approximately 242,000 jobs in 1988. Most worked in hospitals; others worked in independent laboratories, physicians' offices, clinics, health maintenance organizations, public health agencies, pharmaceutical firms, and research institutions. Employment opportunities look good through the year 2000 because of the increased volume of testing.

Dental Hygienists

Dental hygienists provide preventive dental care and encourage patients to develop good oral hygiene skills. They generally evaluate the patient's dental health; remove calculus, stain, and plaque from above and below the gumline; apply caries-preventive agents such as fluorides and pit and fissure sealants; instruct patients on plaque control; expose and develop dental X rays; place temporary fillings and periodontal dressings; remove sutures; and polish and recontour amalgam restorations.

Dental hygienists held approximately 91,000 jobs in 1988. Most dental hygienists work in private dental offices. Others work in public health agencies, school systems, business firms, hospitals, and clinics. Because of the demand of dental care, employment is expected to grow about as fast as the average for all occupations through the year 2000.

Dispensing Opticians

Dispensing opticians order the necessary ophthalmic laboratory work, help the customer select appropriate frames, and adjust the finished eyeglasses. Dispensing opticians measure the corneas of customers' eyes to fit contact lenses which requires considerably more skill, care, and patience than fitting eyeglasses.

Dispensing opticians held approximately 49,000 jobs in 1988. Employment opportunities should be excellent for all levels of dispensing opticians.

EEG Technologists

EEG technologists measure the electrical activity of the brain to help diagnose the extent of injury for patients suspected of having brain tumors, strokes, toxic/metabolic disorders, or epilepsy; to measure the effects of infectious diseases on the brain; and to determine whether individuals with mental or behavioral problems have an organic impairment such as Alzheimer's disease. They work in neurology laboratories, offices of neurologists and neurosurgeons, group medical practices, health maintenance organizations, urgent care centers, and clinics and psychiatric facilities.

EEG technologists held approximately 6,400 jobs in 1988. EEG technologist positions are expected to grow much faster than the average for all occupations through the year 2000. Job opportunities through the year 2000 are expected to be excellent in offices of neurologists, medical group practices, and health maintenance organizations.

EKG Technicians

EKG technicians operate a machine called an electrocardiograph, which records graphic tracings of heartbeats known as electrocardiograms (EKGs, also called ECGs). Since the equipment is mobile, EKG technicians can record electrocardiograms in a doctor's office, in a hospital cardiology department, or at the patient's bedside. Some EKG technicians schedule appointments, type doctors' interpretations, maintain patients' EKG files, and care for equipment. Most EKG technicians are trained on the job for no more than 4 to 6 weeks for the basic "resting" EKG.

EKG technicians held about 18,000 jobs in 1988. Employment of EKG technicians is expected to grow more slowly than the average for all occupations through the year 2000, though a small number of jobs will grow rapidly. These jobs will be available in offices of cardiologists, cardiology clinics, health maintenance organizations, and other outpatient settings.

Emergency Medical Technicians

EMTs first assess the situation and establish priorities for providing emergency services. In addition to carefully assessing the patient's condition, they try to determine whether the patient has epilepsy, diabetes, or other preexisting medical conditions, so they can provide the correct treatment. Operating under strict guidelines, EMTs give appropriate emergency care consistent with their level of training. This may include opening airways, restoring breathing, controlling bleeding, treating for shock, administering oxygen, immobilizing fractures, bandaging, assisting in childbirth, managing emotionally disturbed patients, treating and resuscitating heart attack victims, and giving initial care to poison and burn victims.

In 1988, there were 76,000 paid EMTs. Employment of EMTs is expected to grow about as fast as the average for all occupations through the year 2000. Opportunities for paid EMTs are expected to be best in municipal governments and private ambulance services.

Licensed Practical Nurses

LPNs or LVNs help care for the sick under the direction of physicians and registered nurses. Most LPNs provide basic bedside care. They take such vital signs as temperature, blood pressure, pulse and respiration, and treat bedsores, administer cardiopulmonary resuscitation, prepare and give injections, apply dressings, and insert catheters. They also help patients with bathing and personal hygiene, keep them comfortable, and care for their emotional needs.

Licensed practical nurses held approximately 626,000 jobs in 1988. About half of all LPNs worked in hospitals, and one fifth worked in nursing homes. The rest worked in clinics and doctors' offices, or for temporary help agencies. Employment of LPNs is expected to increase rapidly through the year 2000 in response to the long-term care needs of a growing aged population.

Medical Record Technicians

Medical record technicians are the people who actually handle the records including patient's medical history, results of physical examinations, reports of X-ray and laboratory tests, diagnosis and treatment plans, doctors' orders and notes, and nurses' notes. This job involves teamwork of *medical record administrators, medical record technicians, medical record clerks,* and *medical transcriptionists.* Technicians may also, for example, tabulate and analyze data at the request of hospital officials responsible for quality assurance, marketing, or planning.

Technicians also maintain health record indexes and compile administrative and health statistics for public health officials, administrators, planners, and others.

Medical record technicians held about 47,000 jobs in 1988. Three out of five jobs were in hospitals. Most of the remainder were in medical group practices, health maintenance organizations, nursing homes, clinics, and other facilities that deliver health care. In addition, insurance firms, accounting firms, and law firms that specialize in health matters employ medical record technicians to tabulate and analyze data from medical records. Public health departments hire technicians to supervise data collection from health care institutions and to assist in research. Employment opportunities for medical record technicians are excellent through the year 2000.

Nuclear Medicine Technologists

Nuclear medicine is the branch of radiology that uses radionuclides—unstable atoms that emit radiation spontaneously—in the diagnosis and treatment of disease. Nuclear medicine technologists prepare the radiopharmaceutical for the patient to take, administer it, and then operate the diagnostic imaging equipment to detect and map the radioactive drug in the patient's body to create an image. Nuclear medicine technologists also must be proficient in clinical laboratory procedures.

Nuclear medicine technologists held about 10,000 jobs in 1988. Nearly 9 out of 10 jobs were in hospitals. The rest were in medical laboratories, physicians' offices, outpatient clinics, and imaging centers. Employment is expected to grow faster than the average for all occupations through the year 2000 in response to the health care needs of a growing and aging population.

Radiologic Technologists

Radiologic technologists take X-ray films (radiographs) of all parts of the human body for use in diagnosing medical problems. They prepare patients for radiologic examinations including surrounding the exposed area with radiation protection devices. Because technologists may work with patients who cannot help themselves, good health, moderate strength, and stamina are important. The possibility always exists that patients will have breathing difficulties or go into shock or cardiac arrest; should this happen, the technologists must be ready to assist until other medical personnel can be called in.

Radiologic technologists held approximately 132,000 jobs in 1988. About 3 out of 5 jobs are in hospitals. The rest are located in physicians' offices, health maintenance organizations, clinics, and diagnostic imaging centers. Radiology is a dynamic field with vast clinical potential, and current as well as new uses of imaging equipment are virtually certain to increase demand for radiologic technologists through the year 2000.

Surgical Technologists

Surgical technologists work with, and under the supervision of, surgeons or registered nurses. They help set up the operating room with surgical instruments, equipment, sterile linens, and fluids such as saline or glucose. They may prepare patients for surgery by washing, shaving, and disinfecting body areas where the surgeon will operate. They may transport patients to the operating room and help drape them and position them on the operating table; assist surgeons during surgery; help transfer patients to the recovery room; and assist nurses in cleaning and stocking the operating room for the next operation.

Surgical technologists held about 35,000 jobs in 1988. Employment prospects for graduates of accredited programs in surgical technology are expected to be very good through the year 2000.

JOB DESCRIPTIONS TO KEY HEALTH DIAGNOSING OCCUPATIONS

Chiropractors

Chiropractors are health practitioners who diagnose, treat, and work to prevent diseases, disorders, and injuries to patients whose primary health problems are associated with the body's structural and neurological systems, especially the spine. The standard routine for diagnosis includes taking the patient's medical history, conducting physical, neurological, and orthopedic examinations, ordering laboratory tests, taking X rays, and employing a postural and spinal analysis unique to chiropractic diagnosis. Treatment may involve manually manipulating or adjusting the spinal column, physiological therapeutics, and counseling. The chiropractic approach to health care reflects a holistic view, which stresses the patient's overall well-being. It recognizes that many factors affect health, including exercise, diet, rest, environment, and heredity. Chiropractors encourage the use of natural, non-drug, nonsurgical health treatments.

In 1988, about 36,000 persons practiced chiropractic. Chiropractic practitioners may encounter competition in this growing field.

Dentists

Dentists diagnose and treat problems of the teeth and tissues of the mouth. The practice of dentistry is changing as a result of changes in the dental care needs of the population, greater use of support personnel, and technological advances that affect the materials and techniques dentists employ. A growing percentage of young dentists are preparing for specialty practice. Dentists that are in private practice must handle the business aspects of running an office as well as diagnose and treat dental disease.

Dentists held about 167,000 jobs in 1988. Almost 9 out of 10 dentists are in private practice. Others do research, teach, hold positions in dental schools, or work in hospitals and clinics. Employment of dentists is expected to grow about as fast as the average for all occupations through the year 2000 as changes in population size and structure boost demand for preventive and restorative dentistry.

Optometrists

Optometrists are primary eye care providers who examine people's eyes to diagnose and treat vision problems and, in some cases, eye disease. Those in private practice are also responsible for entire business and office management.

Optometrists held about 37,000 jobs in 1988. Demand for optometric services is expected to grow as fast as the average for all occupations through the year 2000 due to greater recognition of the importance of vision care on the part of the population.

Physicians

Physicians perform medical examinations, diagnose illnesses, treat people suffering from injury or disease and advise patients on good health practices. Medical specialty areas where training is available include internal medicine, general surgery, obstetrics and gynecology, psychiatry, pediatrics, radiology, anesthesiology, ophthalmology, pathology, and orthopedic surgery. There are two types of physicians: Doctor of Medicine—MDs and Doctor of Osteopathy—ODs, who place special emphasis on the body's musculoskeletal system. Most MDs specialize, whereas DOs tend to be primary care providers, such as family practitioners.

Physicians held approximately 535,000 jobs in 1988. About 2 out of 3 were in office-based practice, while others were employed in hospitals, HMOs, urgent care centers, surgicenters, public health clinics, and the federal government. Employment is expected to grow faster than average through the year 2000 due to continued expansion of the health care industry.

Podiatrists

Podiatrists diagnose and treat disorders and diseases of the foot and lower leg. Some specialize in surgery. Other specialties are orthopedics and public health. Subspecialty areas include elderly care, sports medicine, diabetic foot care, and primary podiatric medicine, which is considered the family medicine of foot care.

Podiatrists held about 17,000 jobs in 1988. Most were in private practice, others were employed by hospitals, nursing homes, clinics, HMOs, podiatric medical colleges, and public health departments. Employment is expected to grow much faster than the average through the year 2000 as more people turn to podiatrists for foot care due to the growing population of the elderly and increased enthusiasm for sports.

Veterinarians

Veterinarians diagnose medical problems in their animal patients, perform surgery and prescribe and administer medicines and drugs. Most veterinarians are in private practice and treat small companion animals such as dogs, cats, and birds. Others concentrate on larger animals or have a mixed practice of large and small animals. Employers of veterinarians also include federal, state and local governments, international health agencies, colleges of veterinary medicine, medical schools, research laboratories, livestock farms, animal food companies, and pharmaceutical companies.

Veterinarians held about 46,000 jobs in 1988. The job outlook is extremely good for veterinarians with specialty training in the areas of toxicology, laboratory animal medicine, pathology, and faculty at colleges of veterinary medicine. Though employment opportunities are favorable for others through the year 2000, recent graduates are expected to encounter high competition as they set out to establish a clinical practice.

8

Effective Job Search Techniques for a Health Care Position

What is the best way to find a job? Networking. Contact family, friends, and other peers. Let them know you are seeking a job in the health care industry. That will start the ball rolling. Chances are someone will know someone who is either looking for an employee like yourself or knows of a position coming up.

Another great place to look for jobs is through your national association's trade journal. In Chapter 10, I've listed more than 70 associations and trade journals that have the largest memberships in the health care and medical industry. You'll also find listings of thousands of associations and trade journals in the reference section of your local public library. Large and medium-sized hospitals, clinics, or organizations located throughout the nation as well as smaller organizations will advertise nationally in trade journals with employment opportunities in professions for all types and levels of nurses, therapists, technologists, and administrators, just to name a few. In fact, most professions have a trade journal, book, magazine, and/or newsletter. Ask your librarian for the name of the trade journal that would cover your profession. For example, if you would like to work for a hospital as an EEG technologist, the *American Journal of EEG Technologists* is published by the American Society of Electroneurodiagnostic Technologists (ASET). Each monthly issue lists many jobs, from entry-level to high-level director positions, under "Announcements" at the back of the journal.

Another effective job search technique is to mail your resume directly to the person in charge of the unit or department where you'd like to work, as well as the Human Resources Department. Look in the yellow pages of your local phone directory to see what's available in your area. The public library has yellow page directories of most cities nationwide. First, contact the person in charge of the unit to find out if a position is open or if an opening is likely in the near future. Let him or her know of your interest in the position and to expect to receive your resume in the next day or so. Get the correct spelling and job title of your contact person's name. Send your resume directly to that person. Always follow up with a phone call three days later to verify that your resume was received and to ask if the contact person would like to set up an interview. At this time, he or she will contact the Human Resources Department to arrange an interview. This procedure will definitely speed up your job search process. You may even find that the person in charge of your unit likes certain qualities you possess that the personnel screener may not have seen in the initial screening process of your resume.

Always check your local Sunday classified ads to see *who is* advertising as well. You may find a position available that interests you.

EXECUTIVE SEARCH FIRMS

Executive search firms, also known as executive recruiting or "headhunting" firms, are generally useful if you are seeking a job or position with a salary greater than the $40 thousand per annum. These firms are retained by employers, and as such, never charge you, the applicant, a fee. What kind of positions do these firms generally "headhunt" for? Anything from college presidents and professors, to corporate middle- to executive-level management, scientists, hospital directors, you name it.

The firms act on a retainer. Usually, they structure a contract for a specified number of months in order to conduct a "search." They're paid for their time searching, whether they fill the position or not. Of course, if they do, they may earn a bonus.

A headhunter will probably be more beneficial to you if you are gainfully employed, though interested in seeing what's available at other organizations. In other words, you're better off being pursued than doing the pursuing. However, if your experience and income level warrant it, by all means contact one or two of these firms. They're always interested in adding to their database of quality leads.

SPECIALIZED RECRUITING FIRMS

This group covers a wide middle range of positions in the health care industry. You definitely should contact one to three of these firms if your desired position falls under this category. Even though some of them may use the words "executive" or "search" in their name, they work strictly on a contingency basis. That is, they're paid only if they fill the position.

Here's the key in working with a contingency agency. Select one or more that specialize in your field. They will have more of the appropriate contacts because they'll be marketing themselves to their clients (the employers) as "specialists" in XYZ personnel. But be careful. If they talk about charging *you* a fee, leave. The reputable recruiting agencies are paid 100 percent by client companies.

For further information and listings of Executive Search Firms, contact your local librarian. I found valuable books with listings of 2,000 executive search firms nationwide at the Reference Desk of our public library. Many of these firms specialize in the health care industry.

The National Job Campaigning Resource Center is another great resource if you are interested in specialized executive search firms. They have a wide assortment of directories, at least one of which should help you get started. Both contingency and noncontingency (those that work for a retainer) firms are cataloged.

The directories are up to date and are classified by profession within the health care industry and by geographical location. In addition, they separate contingency from noncontingency firms. You can contact the Center by calling Kenneth J. Cole, Publisher at (904) 235-3733 for a free copy of the information or call the 24-hour order line at (800) 634-4548 or write to PO Box 9433 Panama City Beach, FL 32407. If you mention this book, Kenneth will send you a free copy of *The Recruiting & Search Report*.

EMPLOYMENT AGENCIES

If you work in a less specialized area of health care, the employment agency may very well be of help. Who uses employment agencies? Clerical workers, such as admitting clerks, medical transcriptionists, receptionists, and hospital attendants, to mention a few. Employment agencies offer permanent as well as temporary placement.

The agency offers permanent placement on a contingency basis and may charge you a percentage of its fee. This often amounts to anywhere from one third to one half of your first month's salary. The organization makes up the difference. Some employment agencies will charge you the full fee which usually amounts to your first month's salary. This may seem a little unfair in that those who can least afford it pay a fee. But remember, your competition is going to be much greater.

Temporary placement not only gives you the opportunity to work in many different office environments but allows you the time to find an organization you'd like to work for. Many employers who use temporary help often hire full-time employees through such services.

PROFESSIONAL JOB-CHANGING SERVICES

During the previous decade a new category of professional employment service emerged—the job-changing or outplacement firm. These firms, sometimes one-person shops, go by such classifications as career consultants or counselors, employment or outplacement consultants, management consultants, even career or management psychologists. As such, they will differ widely in their services offered. Some will prepare resumes. Others will train you in effective interviewing techniques. Still others will offer personality and skills inventory testing. Some may even offer to make a few contacts for you. What you get will depend on the firm and how much you're willing to spend. Yes—they will charge you, and probably dearly, for their time.

When, if ever, should you consider using one of these firms? Realistically, when you're ready to make a real career change. In other words, you have business or professional experience, but not in the field you want to break into. Or maybe you're at a point in your career (like so many before you) where you don't know what it is you want to do with the rest of your life. In such an instance, the career or employment counselor could be of great help.

Incidentally, the term "outplacement" is one you should become familiar with. It refers to the practice of companies attempting to find alternative employment usually for middle- to upper-level management.

TRADE AND PROFESSIONAL ASSOCIATIONS

Are you now in or ready to begin a career in a specialized field of the health care industry? Anything from nursing, medical technology, sports medicine, speech therapy, to you-name-it? If you are, don't overlook the importance of joining one or more trade or professional associations. What value do such groups have?

1. *Information.* These organizations often serve as clearing-houses for inside industry information. They also publish trade journals, "Who's Who" directories, notices of various conventions, and so forth. The information you'll gain makes this a smart way of keeping up with what's happening in your chosen field.

2. *People.* Networking—the art of letting people know who you are—can often make the difference in getting the job you want or in making that upward career move. The more contacts you have, the more potential opportunities exist for career advancement. The adage that "it's not what you know but who you know" has some merit when job searching.

Again, the Reference Desk at your local library is a wonderful source for finding the professional association just for you. I've seen books at our local library that list thousands of associations nationwide. Again, in Chapter 10, I've listed more than 70 associations that have the largest memberships in the health care and medical professions.

If you're excited about your chosen field of endeavor and are open to relocating in the future for the right career opportunity, consider joining a professional association to help take you there.

9

Preparing for the Interview in the Health Care Profession

Going on an interview can be both nerve-racking and exciting. Here are some helpful hints to think about before the interview. Following these suggestions can greatly reduce your tension level.

1. Call the hospital or organization and ask for information. In the interview, when you are asked if you know about the organization, it is very impressive to mention various aspects of the business. A little bit of research can go a long way.

Tip: Know the *philosophy* of the institution—what they believe in. Know their *Mission Statement*—the direction they are headed. For example, one hospital administrator told me their mission is to be the top regional health care center in the state of Colorado.

You can call or write to the hospital Human Resources Department and ask for this specific information before going to the interview.

Tip: Always schedule an appointment for an interview. Scheduling time with the recruiter demonstrates professionalism.

2. For out-of-town organizations, check with the reference librarian of your public library for more information about the hospital, clinic, or organization.

3. Bring three or four resumes with you to the interview. You could be interviewed by one to three employers. Hand a resume to each interviewer and always keep one for yourself. Chances are the interviewer will use your resume to interview you, and this will make the experience go a lot smoother for everyone. It's permissible to refer to your resume during the interview, though I suggest you try to memorize the main points beforehand.

4. Always bring a pad of paper and pen to the interview. Ask questions about the job and take notes. You may want to jot down a few questions before you go on the interview. Also, remember to write the interviewer's name and title (with the correct spelling) on your notepad to address a thank you letter after the interview.

Tip: It is very impressive to most recruiters that you came prepared for the interview. It demonstrates to them just how serious you are about the job.

5. Remember, think positive! Focus on your strengths. Talk about what you do have to offer, not what you don't. If you're applying for a position you do not have experience in yet, focus on enthusiasm and eagerness to learn. Do not even think about your lack of experience. Enthusiasm is a great asset that employers notice. Sometimes the employer would rather train an enthusiastic employee with no experience than hire an experienced employee who lacks that quality. We all know that most health care professionals already have to go through many years of specialized training. Many health care employers are seeking a trained professional for a specific position who is people oriented with the ability to react quickly to emergency situations in a calm and controlled manner. If you can demonstrate to them that you possess this quality in yourself, it is likely that you'll get the job.

6. A desire for job security is also something most employers like to hear. It confirms in their minds that you really are planning to stay with the organization for a decent amount of time. But most importantly it provides a bond that is mutually beneficial for both parties—employer and employee.

7. After the interview, immediately send a personalized thank you letter to the potential employer.

TOUGH QUESTIONS MOST ASKED IN A HOSPITAL INTERVIEW AND THE ANSWERS THE INTERVIEWER WANTS TO HEAR

Nursing

Q. What do you see for your unit in 5 years? (This is a hot topic for the 1990s.)

A. A practice model where physicians and nurses are equal. A self-governance model where the staff nurses form committees and they decide what to do for their unit.

Q. How would you handle a conflict resolution with your physician?

A. Speak to the physician about it directly. If it's personal, work it out within myself.

Q. How do you handle coping skills after an emergency?

A. After everything is okay, I'll take a break and walk around the hospital. When it's time to go home, I might take the scenic route home, go to an aerobics class, eat a favorite cookie, pray, meditate, or take a walk by the ocean. It depends on what feels right to me.

Q. What is the biggest issue facing nursing today?

A. Demonstrating accountability for yourself and being recognized as a professional.

Q. What can you bring to our organization?

A. Good communication skills with physicians, patients, and other staff members through self-esteem and feeling proud of what I do in my job.

Q. Describe your strengths and weaknesses?

A. My strength is my ability to communicate well with physicians, patients, and other staff members and being self-motivated and organized with the ability to handle highly stressful situations quickly and calmly. My weaknesses are I don't write well, but I did have an article published. And, I don't have much experience with budgeting, but I am a quick learner.

Q. How do you feel about getting paid salary instead of hourly? (This is a new concept in the health care industry.

All hospital units across the country are turning to salaried position with any 4-year degree professional position.)

A. (This is not optional. But *do* ask about the pros and cons.)

Clinical Nurse Specialist

Q. What can you do for our organization to promote quality care?

A. Capitalize on reliability, self-motivation, and organization. I would present ideas of how to make the program better with a cost-effective approach. (Then try to turn the interview around. Ask the interviewer this. Are there any restrictions for program implementation? Will I have the budgetary and administrative support I need to get the job done?)

Home Care Nursing

Q. What do you think is the toughest part of this job? What are the negatives?

A. 1. Lack of day-to-day peer group. 2. Lots of paperwork. 3. Medicare rules and regulations.

Cardiology Catheterization Lab Nurse

Q. After watching these procedures, are you willing to learn all that's involved?

A. Yes. (Keep in mind this is a very technical, specialized, and critical unit that is not taught in nursing school. It can be intimidating.)

Nurse, Birthing Unit

Q. What would you do if you disagreed with a physician's diagnosis and/or plan of treatment?

A. Follow the unit's policy for concurrent audits.

Staff Developmental Coordinator, Critical Care Nursing

Q. How effective is your teaching?

A. My teaching has proven to be very effective as demonstrated through my students and staff members.

Q. Give me an example of your critical decision-making skills. How do you teach this?

A. (Be prepared to give an example of a teaching curriculum as well.)

Radiology Technologist

Q. How do you feel about the risk factor involved with radiation?

A. In any job, there's a certain amount of risk. You perform necessary precautions so that you don't put yourself, your co-workers, or your patients at risk.

Rehabilitation Aide

Q. What would you do if you have a stroke patient having a difficult time getting dressed.

A. Be very patient with him or her. Demonstrate patience by giving lots of encouragement and verbal coaching that will help the person dress himself or herself.

Infection Control Coordinator

Q. How do you approach the physician who has a patient with a hospital-acquired infection?

A. Talk to the physician directly. Ask if he can identify any common factors regarding the infection that would indicate the reason the patient got the infection.

Q. What do you tell a patient who has a hospital-acquired infection?

A. Explain to the patient that everyone has bacteria on their skin and a small percentage of people will develop an infection. The important thing to do is recognize it and treat it quickly.

EEG Technologist

Q. Can you do Evoked Potentials?

A. Yes (or no, but I'm willing to learn). Some hospitals will train you.

Q. Are you capable of monitoring in surgery?

A. Yes. (Give an example of having done it.)

Q. Can you insert nasopharyngeal electrodes?

A. Yes (or no, but I'm willing to learn). Larger hospitals will require you to do this, but it can be taught on the job.

Q. What other kinds of testing can you do?

A. Brain mapping; ambulatory EEG; All night sleep studies; ASLTs.

Medical Technologist

Q. How would you deal with a mistake you made on a test that's been reported?

A. I would know right away and tell the doctor immediately that an error has occurred and that the test will be repeated.

Q. How do you deal with difficult-to-handle patients; for example, needing to draw blood twice in a sitting?

A. I would be patient with the client and act in a professional and concerned manner to console him or her while explaining the necessity of the test. If I need to repeat the test more than twice or anytime I feel it necessary, I will ask for assistance.

Q. If you were going to run a routine swab specimen for a virus test, what does the holding medium have to contain?

A. Antibiotics.

Respiratory Therapist, Respiratory Care Unit

Q. Tell me what you know about the equipment you need to operate?

A. (Be prepared to answer this kind of technical question. Know your equipment.)

Pediatric Physical/Occupational Therapist (Preschool Setting)

Q. What would you do if there is a child whose parents don't want therapy services but you clearly see the child needs therapy?

A. Work with the parents who are in the process of denial. Offer them more information on therapy as well as counseling resources.

Medical Social Worker

Q. What is your theory of being able to assess people? How would you apply this to the job?

A. (Be prepared to be concrete. Think of an example of how you've applied your theory to someone you've actually worked with.)

Q. What are your strengths and weaknesses?

A. My strength is the ability to communicate well with all types of people. My biggest weakness is I work too hard. And, even though I turn in my paperwork on time, I have a difficult time filling it out sometimes.

Q. Can you describe a conflict and how you would resolve it?

A. (Demonstrate flexibility skills. Be prepared to talk about a specific conflict that you were involved in that ended up satisfying all parties.)

QUESTIONS FOR YOU TO ASK THE INTERVIEWER

1. What is your turnover rate for nursing (or your own profession?)

2. What is your usage rate of registry or agency staff and traveling nurses?

3. What kind of advancement opportunities do you have to offer?

4. Does the hospital (or other health care facility) provide in-services and continued educational opportunities or do I have to go outside? For example, do they offer certification in specialty areas?

5. Is the facility accredited? (Not all facilities are accredited.)

6. Before you get offered a position, always ask if you can speak to staff members about the job.

7. Does the facility offer incentive programs? For instance, is there a relocation package if you are hired from out-of-state? (I know of hospitals that do not offer incentive programs but do offer great educational opportunities, and provide in-services, excellent benefit package, advancement opportunities, and certification programs. Their turnover rate for nurses is less than 1 percent.)

REMEMBER: JOB SATISFACTION, BENEFIT PACKAGE, PHILOSOPHY, AND QUALITY OF CARE CAN BE WORTH A LOT MORE THAN AN INCENTIVE PROGRAM.

LIST OF REFERENCES AND LETTERS OF RECOMMENDATION

Most employers will ask for three personal and/or business references. References are simply the listing of names, with professional title, organization worked for, organization address, and phone number of those who will give you a reference. Always let your contacts know prior to using their names as a reference that you plan to do so and make sure they will give you a *good* one. It is usually unnecessary to mail references with your resume and cover letter unless requested. It is however, a good idea to bring them with you to the interview along with a letter of recommendation. A letter of recommendation is the letter written by a previous employer on the company stationery, highly recommending you for the position. If the letter doesn't include such a recommendation, don't use it.

WHAT TO WEAR FOR THE INTERVIEW

Always dress up for an interview. Your appearance will be the interviewer's first impression of you. Women should wear a nice dress or skirt and blouse; men should wear a suit and tie. Even if you know the organization's employees dress casually on the job, you are not an employee, yet. You want to look businesslike and professional. Dressing up for the interview shows the employer you take your work seriously. Believe me, it will make a difference.

10

List of Health Care and Medical Associations and Publications

American College of Cardiology
9111 Old Georgetown Road
Bethesda, MD 20814
(800) 253-4636

Membership as of 1991: 18,000

Publications: *ACCEL*, monthly; *Affiliates in Training*, quarterly; *Cardiology*, monthly; *Journal of the American College of Cardiology*, 14/year.

American Heart Association
7320 Greenville Avenue
Dallas, TX 75231
(214) 373-6300

Membership as of 1991: 200,000

Publications: *Arteriosclerosis and Thrombosis: A Journal of Vascular Biology*, bimonthly; *Cardiovascular Nursing*, bimonthly; *Circulation*, monthly; *Circulation Research*, monthly; *Current Concepts of Cerebrovascular Disease and Stroke*, bimonthly; *Hypertension*, monthly; *Modern Concepts of Cardiovascular Disease*, monthly; *Stroke—A Journal of Cerebral Circulation*, monthly.

National Association of Dental Assistants
900 S. Washington Street, No. G-13
Falls Church, VA 22046
(703) 237-8616
Membership as of 1991: 5,000
Publication: *The Explorer*, monthly.

American Dental Assistants Association
919 N. Michigan Avenue, Suite 3400
Chicago, IL 60611
(312) 664-3327
Membership as of 1991: 15,000
Publication: *The Dental Assistant*, bimonthly.

American Dental Association
211 E. Chicago Avenue
Chicago, IL 60611
(312) 440-2500
Membership as of 1991: 140,000
Publications: *American Dental Directory*, annual; *Index to Dental Literature*, quarterly.

American Dental Hygienists' Association
444 N. Michigan Avenue, Suite 3400
Chicago, IL 60611
(312) 440-8929
Membership as of 1991: 30,000
Publications: *American Dental Hygienists' Association Access*, 10/year; *Dental Hygiene*, 9/year.

National Board of Certification in Dental Technology
3801 Mt. Vernon Avenue
Alexandria, VA 22305
(703) 683-5310
Certificants as of 1991: 10,400
Publication: *Who's Who in the Dental Laboratory Industry*, annual.

American Board of Certified and Registered
Encephalographic Technicians and Technologists (EEG)
Neurodiagnostic Department
Mercy Hospital and Medical Center
4077 Fifth Avenue
San Diego, CA 92103-2180
(619) 294-8111
Membership as of 1991: 1,200.

American Board of Registration of EEG Technologists
PO Box 11434
Norfolk, VA 23417
(804) 627-5503
Nonmembership

American Gastroenterological Association
6900 Grove Road
Thorofare, NJ 08086
(609) 848-9218
Membership as of 1991: 6,400
Publications: *AGA Membership Roster,* annual; *AGA News,* quarterly;
Gastroenterology, monthly; *Viewpoints of Digestive Diseases,* 5/year.

American Medical Technologists
710 Higgins Road
Park Ridge, IL 60068
(708) 823-5169
Membership as 1991: 22,150
Publications: *AMT Events and Continuing Education Supplement,* 8/
year; *Manual of the Accrediting Bureau of Health Education Schools.*

American Registry of Radiologic Technologists
1255 Northland Drive
Mendota Heights, MN 55120
(612) 687-0048
Membership as of 1991: 180,000
Publication: *Annual Director of Registered Technologists,* every 3 years.

American Society for Medical Technology
2021 L Street, NW, Suite 400
Washington, DC 20036
(202) 785-3311

Membership as of 1991: 20,000

Publications: *ASMT Statements*, quarterly; *ASMT Today*, bimonthly; *Clinical Laboratory Science*, bimonthly.

American Society of Radiologic Technologists
15000 Central Avenue SE
Albuquerque, NM 87123
(505) 298-4500

Membership as of 1991: 16,000

Publications: *ASRT Scanner*, bimonthly; *Radiologic Technology*, bimonthly.

Association of Surgical Technologists
8307 Shaffer Parkway
Littleton, CO 80127
(303) 978-9010/(800) 637-7433

Membership as of 1991: 11,500

Publications: *AST News*, bimonthly; *Directory of Certified Surgical Technologists*, annual; *The Surgical Technologist*, bimonthly; *Study and Test Skills for Health Professionals and AST Core Curriculum*.

International Society for Clinical Laboratory Technology
818 Olive, Suite 918
St. Louis, MO 63101
(314) 241-1445

Membership as of 1991: 7,500

Publication: *ISCLT Newsletter*, bimonthly.

National Association of Orthopaedic Technologists
PO Box 1829
Martinez, CA 94553
(415) 943-6434

Membership as of 1991: 1,000

Publication: *OnLine Communications*, bimonthly.

National Certification Agency for Medical Lab Personnel
2021 L Street NW, Suite 400
Washington, DC 20036
(202) 857-1023

Membership as of 1991: 44,000

National Society for Histotechnology
5900 Princess Garden Parkway, Suite 805
Lanham, MD 20706
(301) 577-4907

Membership as of 1991: 3,000

Publications: *Annual Report; Journal of Histotechnology,* quarterly; *NSH in Action,* quarterly; also publishes training aids, career booklets, and film.

American Association of Medical Society Executives
515 N. State Street
Chicago, IL 60610
(312) 464-2555

Membership as of 1991: 1,000

Publications: *Hotline,* monthly; *The Medical Executive,* quarterly; *Who's Who in Medical Society Management,* annual.

Nuclear Medicine Technology Certification Board
2970 Clairmont Road, Suite 610
Atlanta, GA 30329
(404) 315-1739

Membership as of 1991: 12,000

Publications: *Certification Examination Validation Report,* annual; *Director,* annual; *Examination Report,* annual.

Society of Nuclear Medicine
136 Madison Avenue, 8th Floor
New York, NY 10016-6760
(212) 889-0717

Membership as of 1991: 12,200

Publications: *The Journal of Nuclear Medicine,* monthly; *Journal of Nuclear Medicine Technology,* quarterly; *Newsline,* quarterly; *Society of Nuclear Medicine Membership Director,* every 3 years.

American Association of Nurse Anesthetists
216 W. Higgins Road
Park Ridge, IL 60068-5790
(708) 692-7050

Membership as of 1991: 23,000

Publications: *AANA Journal*, bimonthly; *AANA Newsbulletin Bulletin*, monthly; *American Association of Nurse Anesthetists List of Recognized Educational Programs*, semiannual.

American Board of Neuroscience Nursing (ABNN)
c/o Professional Examination Service
475 Riverside Drive
New York, NY 10115
(212) 870-3248

Membership as of 1991: 765

Publication: *Role Delineation Study of Neuroscience Nursing.*

American Association of Occupational Health
50 Lenox Pointe
Atlanta, GA 30324
(404) 262-1162

Membership as of 1991: 11,500

Publications: *Journal*, monthly; *Newsletter*, monthly.

American Licensed Practical Nurses Association
1090 Vermonth Avenue, NW, Suite 1200
Washington, DC 20005
(202) 682-5800

Membership as of 1991: 6,200

Publications: Pamphlets and papers of legislation and nursing standards.

American Nurses' Association
2420 Pershing Road
Kansas City, MO 64108
(202) 554-4444

Membership as of 1991: 200,000

Publications: *American Journal of Nursing*, monthly; *Annual Report*; *Facts About Nursing*, semiannual; *Proceedings of the House of Delegates*, annual.

American Nursing Assistant's Association
PO Box 103
Ottawa, KS 66067-0103
Membership as of 1991: 210
Publication: *Nursing Notes*, 2/year.

American Organization of Nurse Executives
AHA Building
840 N. Lake Shore Drive
Chicago, IL 60611
(312) 280-4190
Membership as of 1991: 5,500
Publication: *Nurse Executive*, monthly.

American Society of Ophthalmic Registered Nurses (ASORN)
PO Box 193030
San Francisco, CA 94119
(415) 561-8513
Membership as of 1991: 1,800
Publication: *American Society of Ophthalmic Registered Nurses—Insight*, bimonthly.

American Society of Plastic and Reconstructive
Surgical Nurses (ASPRSN)
Box 56, N. Woodbury Road
Pitman, NJ 08071
(609) 589-6247
Membership as of 1991: 1,200
Publications: *ASPRSN Membership Directory*, annual; *ASPRS News*, bimonthly; *Plastic Surgical Nursing*, quarterly.

American Society of Post Anesthesia Nurses (ASPAN)
11512 Allecingie Parkway
Richmond, VA 23235
(804) 379-5516
Membership as of 1991: 6,600
Publications: *Breathline*, bimonthly; *Journal of Postanesthesia Nursing*, bimonthly.

Dermatology Nurses' Association (DNA)
Box 56, N. Woodbury Road
Pitman, NJ 08071
(609) 582-1915

Membership as of 1991: 1,323

Publications: *DNA Membership Directory*, annual; *Newsletter*, bimonthly; *Product Guide*, annual.

Federation for Accessible Nursing Education and Licensure (FANEL)
2033 Sixth Avenue, No. 804
Seattle, WA 98122
(206) 441-6020

Publication: *Newsletter*, bimonthly.

NAACOG Certification Corporation
645 N. Michigan Avenue, Suite 1058
Chicago, IL 60611
(312) 951-0207

Publication: *NCC News*, periodic.

NAACOG: The Organization for Obstetric, Gynecologic, and Neonatal Nurses
409 12th Street, SW
Washington, DC 20024
(202) 638-0026

Membership as of 1991: 24,000

Publications: *Journal of Obstetric, Gynecologic, and Neonatal Nursing*, bimonthly; *NAACOG Newsletter*, monthly.

National Association of Orthopaedic Nurses (NAON)
Box 56 N. Woodbury Road
Pitman, NJ 08071
(609) 582-0111

Membership as of 1991: 8,500

Publications: *News*, bimonthly; *Orthopaedic Nursing*, bimonthly.

National Association of Pediatric Nurse Associates and Practitioners (NAPNAP)
1101 Kings Highway N., No. 206
Cherry Hills, NJ 08034
(609) 667-1773

Membership as of 1991: 3,100

Publications: *Journal of Pediatric Health Care*, bimonthly; *Pediatric Nurse Practitioner*, bimonthly.

National League for Nursing
350 Hudson Street
New York, NY 10014
(212) 989-9393

Membership as of 1991: 19,800

Publications: *Newsletter*, periodic; *Nurse Faculty Census*, biennial; *Nursing Data Review*, annual; *Nursing and Health Care*, 10/year; *Nursing Student Census*, annual; *Public Policy Bulletin*, periodic; *State Approved Schools of Nursing—LPN*, annual; *State Approved Schools of Nursing—RN*, annual.

National Organization for Advancement of Associate Degree Nursing (NOAADN)
2033 Sixth Avenue, Suite 804
Seattle, WA 98121
(206) 441-6020

Membership as of 1991: 4,000

Publications: *AD Nurse Journal*, periodic; *Newsletter*, quarterly.

North American Nursing Diagnosis Association (NANDA)
3525 Caroline Street
St. Louis, MO 63104
(314) 577-8954

Membership as of 1991: 1,500

Publications: *Conference Proceedings*, biennial; *Nursing Diagnosis Journal*, quarterly.

Nurse Consultants Association (NCA)
414 Plaza Drive, Suite 209
Westmont, IL 60559
(708) 655-0087

Membership as of 1991: 150

Publications: *Membership Directory*, semiannual; *Newsletter*, quarterly.

American Dietetic Association
216 Jackson Boulevard, Suite 800
Chicago, IL 60606
(312) 899-0040

Membership as of 1991: 60,000

Publication: *Journal of the American Dietetic Association*, monthly.

Association of State and Territorial Public Health Nutrition Directors (ASTPHND)
Pennsylvania Dept. of Health, Div. of Health Promotion
Health Welfare Building, Room 103
PO Box 90
Harrisburg, PA 17108
(717) 787-6967

Membership as of 1991: 55

Publications: *Annual Membership Director; ASTPHND Newsletter,* 3–4/year.

Consultant Dieticians in Health Care Facilities
216 W. Jackson Boulevard, Suite 800
Chicago, IL 60606
(412) 283-7025

Membership as of 1991: 5,000

Publications: *The Consultant Dietitian,* quarterly; *Membership Directory,* annual.

Dietary Managers Association
400 E. 22nd Street
Lombard, IL 60148
(708) 932-1444

Membership as of 1991: 12,000

Publications: *Flyer,* bimonthly; *Issues,* bimonthly.

Feingold Association of the United States (Nutrition) (FAUS)
PO Box 6550
Alexandria, VA 22306
(703) 768-FAUS

Membership as of 1991: 30,000

Publication: *Pure Facts,* 10/year.

American Society of Consultant Pharmacists
2300 Ninth Street S., Suite 515
Arlington, VA 22204
(703) 920-8492

Membership as of 1991: 3,600

Publications: *Clinical Consult,* quarterly; *Consultant Pharmacists,* monthly; *UPDATE,* monthly.

American Society of Hospital Pharmacists
4630 Montgomery Avenue
Bethesda, MD 20814
(301) 657-3000

Membership as of 1991: 23,000

Publications: *AHFS Drug Information*, annual; *American Journal of Hospital Pharmacy*, monthly; *ASHP Newsletter*, monthly; *Clinical Pharmacy*, monthly; *Handbook on Injectable Drugs*, biennial; *International Pharmaceutical Abstracts*, semimonthly.

Associates of Clinical Pharmacology
2317 International Lane, Suite 210
Madison, WI 53704
(608) 244-1600

Membership as of 1991: 2,600

Publications: *ACP Membership Directory*, annual; *Journal of Clinical Research and Pharmacoepidemiology*, quarterly; *Monitor*, quarterly.

American Academy of Physician Assistants (AAPA)
950 N. Washington Street
Alexandria, VA 22314
(703) 836-2272

Membership as of 1991: 13,000

Publications: *AAPA Bulletin*, monthly; *AAPA News*, monthly; *Journal of the American Academy of Physician Assistants*, bimonthly; *Legislative Watch*, monthly; *Membership Director*, annual; *PAJF Employment Magazine*, biweekly.

American Psychological Association
1200 17th Street, NW
Washington, DC 20036
(202) 955-7600

Membership as of 1991: 70,000

Publications: *American Psychologist*, monthly; *APA Membership Register*, periodic; *APA Monitor*, monthly; *Behavioral Neuroscience*, bimonthly; *Biographical Director*, periodic; *Contemporary Psychology*, monthly; *Developmental Psychology*, bimonthly; *Journal of Abnormal Psychology*; numerous other publications. Call for more information.

National Association for Music Therapy
505 11th Street, SE
Washington, DC 20003
(202) 543-6864

Membership as of 1991: 3,800

Publications: *Journal of Music Therapy,* quarterly; *Music Therapy Clinical Training Facilities Handbook,* biennial; *Music Therapy Perspectives,* annual; *National Association for Music Therapy—Membership Directory,* annual; *Music Therapy Index* (vols. 1 and 2), and *Handbook of Music Psychology.*

National Association of Neuro-Linguistic Programming
310 N. Alabama, Suite A100
Indianapolis, IN 46204
(317) 636-6059

Membership as of 1991: 1,400

Publications: *NA/NLP Membership Directory,* annual; *NA/NLP Newsletter,* quarterly.

National Association of Quality Assurance Professionals (NAQAP)
104 Wilmot, Suite 201
Deerfield, IL 60015
(708) 940-8800

Membership as of 1991: 5,200

Publications: *Journal of Quality Assurance,* bimonthly; *Membership Directory,* annual; *Regional Update Newsletter,* quarterly.

American College of Radiology
1891 Preston White Drive
Reston, VA 22091
(703) 648-8900

Membership as of 1991: 20,000

Publications: *Bulletin,* monthly; *Directory,* annual.

American HealthCare Radiology Administrators
PO Box 334
Sudbury, MA 01776
(508) 443-7591

Membership as of 1991: 3,100

Publications: *Announcement,* monthly; *Membership Directory,* annual; *Radiology Management,* quarterly; *Bibliography for the Radiology Administrator.*

American Institute of Ultrasound in Medicine
4405 East-West Highway, Suite 504
Bethesda, MD 20814
(301) 656-6117

Membership as of 1991: 8,800

Publications: *AIUM Annual Convention Proceedings; AIUM Membership Directory*, biennial; *AIUM Newsletter*, monthly; *Journal of Ultrasound in Medicine*, monthly.

American Registry of Diagnostic Medical Sonographers
2368 Victory Parkway, No. 510
Cincinnati, OH 45206-2810
(513) 281-7111

Membership as of 1991: 11,000

Publications: *American Registry of Diagnostic Medical Sonographers Director*, annual; *Informational Brochure*, annual.

Society of Diagnostic Medical Sonographers
12225 Greenville Avenue, Suite 434
Dallas, TX 75243
(214) 235-7367

Membership as of 1991: 7,600

Publications: *Journal of Diagnostic Medical Sonography*, biennial; *Newsletter*, biennial; *1989 Compensation Survey, Director of Education, Guidelines for Student Review*.

American Ear Association for Research (AEAR)
32 Sterling Road
Mt. Pocono, PA 18344
(717) 839-3332

Membership as of 1991: 10,000

Publication: *AEAR Newsletter*, semiannual.

American Speech-Language-Hearing Association (ASHA)
10801 Rockville Pike
Rockville, MD 20852
(301) 897-5700

Membership as of 1991: 60,000

Publications: *Asha*, monthly; *ASHA Monographs*, periodic; *ASHA Reports*, periodic; *Guide to Graduate Education in Speech-Language Pathology and Audiology*, biennial; *Journal of Speech and Hearing Research*, bimonthly; *Language, Speech and Hearing Service in Schools*, quarterly.

American Tinnitus Association
PO Box 5
Portland, OR 97207
(503) 248-9985

Membership as of 1991: 150,000

Publications: *Tinnitus Today*, quarterly; *Tinnitus Bibliography*.

Adventures in Movement for the Handicapped (AIM)
945 Danbury Road
Dayton, OH 45420
(513) 294-4611

Membership as of 1991: 25,000

Publications: *Adventurer*, quarterly; *Adventures in Movement*, semiannual; *Adventures in Movement for the Handicapped Newsletter*, annual.

American Association for Respiratory Care
11030 Ables Lane
Dallas, TX 75229
(214) 243-2272

Membership as of 1991: 27,000

Publications: *AARC Times: The Magazine for the Respiratory Care Professional*, monthly; *Respiratory Care*, monthly.

American Occupational Therapy Association (AOTA)
1383 Piccard Drive, Suite 301
Rockville, MD 20850-4375
(301) 948-9626

Membership as of 1991: 42,000

Publications: *American Journal of Occupational Therapy*, monthly; *Occupational Therapy Week*; *Physical Disabilities Special Interest Section Newsletter*, quarterly; *Sensory Integration Special Interest Section Newsletter*, quarterly.

American Occupational Therapy Certification Board (AOTCB)
1383 Piccard Drive, Suite 105
Rockville, MD 20850
(301) 990-7979

Publications: Brochures and reports explaining certification procedures.

American Physical Therapy Association (APTA)
1111 N. Fairfax Street
Alexandria, VA 22314
(703) 684-2782

Membership as of 1991: 50,000

Publications: *American Physical Therapy Association Progress Report,*
periodic; *Clinical Management in Physical Therapy,* bimonthly; *Physical
Therapy,* monthly; *PT Bulletin,* weekly; *Today's Student PT,* semiannual.

National Board for Respiratory Care
8310 Nieman Road
Lenexa, KS 66214
(913) 599-4200

Membership as of 1991: 90,000

Publications: *Annual Director; Newsletter,* bimonthly.

National Council for Therapeutic Recreation Certification (NCTRC)
49 S. Main Street, Suite 005
Spring Valley, NY 10977
(914) 356-9660

Membership as of 1991: 10,500

Publications: *NCTRC Newsletter,* semiannual; NCTRC Registry, annual.

National Therapeutic Recreation Society
3101 Park Center Drive, 12th Floor
Alexandria, VA 22302
(703) 820-4940

Membership as of 1991: 3,200

Publications: *NTRS Newsletter,* quarterly; *Parks and Recreation,*
monthly; *Therapeutic Recreation Journal,* quarterly.

Orthopaedic Section, American Physical Therapy Association
505 King Street, Suite 103
La Crosse, WI 54601
(608) 784-0910

Membership as of 1991: 10,965

Publications: *Bulletin of the Orthopaedic Section,* quarterly; *Journal of
Orthopaedic and Sports Physical Therapy,* monthly; *Terminology of Orthopaedic Physical Therapy.*

Private Practice Section/American Physical Therapy Association
(PPS)
1101 17th Street, NW, Suite 1000
Washington, DC 20036
(202) 457-1115

Membership as of 1991: 4,500

Publications: *Private Practice Section Membership Director*, annual;
Physical Therapy Today, quarterly; *Twenty Questions about Private Practice; An Employers Guide to Obtaining Physical Therapy Services.*

U.S. Physical Therapy Association (USPTA)
1803 Avon Lane
Arlington Heights, IL 60004

Membership as of 1991: 12,700

Publication: *Journal*, periodic.

American Association of Veterinary Anatomists
Auburn University
College of Veterinary Medicine
Department of Anatomy and Histology
Auburn, AL 36849
(205) 844-6743

Membership as of 1991: 250

Publications: *Directory*, biennial; *Newsletter*, semiannual.

American Association of Zoo Veterinarians (AAZV)
Philadelphia Zoo
34th Street and Girard Avenue
Philadelphia, PA 19104
(215) 387-9094

Membership as of 1991: 800

Publications: *Annual Membership Directory; Annual Conference Proceedings; Journal of Zoo and Wildlife Medicine*, quarterly; *Newsletter*,
quarterly.

11

Resume Samples from More Than 100 Health Care Professionals

The following pages in this chapter include many examples of resumes from the Just Resumes® health care client files. Other samples were prepared specifically for this book. All these resumes offer accurate job descriptions and educational requirement information. Be aware that the educational requirements vary from state to state, and the job titles and descriptions vary for each hospital, clinic, university, or other health care organization.

The following resume samples include professionals from health technologists and technicians, health assessment and treating occupations, and health service occupations, each resume focusing on particular individual goals. You will see a variety of formats to choose from in functional, chronological, and combination styles. There's an index to the resume samples in the back of the book. The resumes are listed in alphabetical order and conveniently categorized by job title.

Look at each resume carefully. Again, think about how your own background applies to the job or internship you'd like to obtain.

Remember, to take full advantage of the valuable information in this book and to give you the overall perspective you'll need to write your own effective resume, it's important that you've already read all the text in Chapters 1 and 2 before reviewing the resume samples in this chapter.

BRENDA HOFFMAN
Licensed Acupuncturist
1257 Olive Street
Summerland, CA 93108
(805) 682-1470

Objective: Acupuncturist

PROFESSIONAL EXPERIENCE

Private & Group Detox-Acupuncture
- Administered in-house acupuncture and herbal treatment for the Skid Row population of 60-150 clients per day.
- Monitored clients with breathilizer and urine testing.
- Provided continued recovery treatment and referral service, working with law enforcement, social services and counselors throughout the community.
- Treated individuals and provided home detox care to private patients.
- Gained life experience participating in family members' drug addiction/recovery process.
- Received "Outstanding Accomplishment" from the Mayor of Los Angeles for participation in the Turnaround Program - January, 1988.

Foreign-Group Therapy/Counseling
- Provided crisis intervention, brief and long term counseling to:
  - individual adults   -adolescents   -couples   -groups
- Dealt with clients of racial and economic diversity.
- Conducted group therapy series utilizing Peer Counseling or Bioenergetic techniques.
- Founding member of a 300 person skill training-work cooperative in London.

EDUCATION
SAMRA Univ. of Oriental Medicine, LA, CA
Doctor of Oriental Medicine, 1986
Bachelor of Science Degree, 1983
Graduate Studies, Beijing, China, 1986
Qi Gong, Acupuncture

SPECIAL TRAINING
- California Acupuncture License #CA 1589 since 1983
- National Acupuncture Detox Assoc, Certified 1986
- Hypnotherapy Certification Board of California, 1983
- First Int'l Qi Gong Conference, Shanghai, China, 1986
- Acupuncture Detox Training Program, Lincoln Hospital, Los Angeles, CA, 1982 & 1986

EMPLOYMENT HISTORY

Clinic Director/Acupuncturist, Wheeler Holistic Clinic, LA, CA	1989-present
Licensed Acupuncturist, Health Spectrum, Santa Barbara, CA	1985-89
Volunteer Acupuncturist, Turnaround (Detox Facility), LA, CA	1979-85

BETH ANNE ELLISON
PO Box 1287
Santa Barbara, CA 93190
(805) 569-9876

OBJECTIVE
An Admitting Clerk Supervisor position

OFFICE SKILLS
Insurance billing...ten key adding machine...data entry... medical terminology...accounts payable & receivable...excellent phone skills...filing. Typing speed: 65 + wpm.

PROFESSIONAL EXPERIENCE
SANTA BARBARA CITY HOSPITAL   1985-present
Admitting Clerk II
- Admit in-patients, out-patients and emergency room patients.
- Schedule future surgeries.
- Verify benefits and receive prior authorizations for Medi-cal and Medicare patients.
- Work closely with insurance companies, doctor's offices and county agencies throughout Santa Barbara county.
- Train new employees.
- Supervise staff members in the absence of department supervisor.

KELCOM MEDICAL SOFTWARE CONSULTANTS, Santa Barbara, CA   1985-88
Administrative Assistant
- Performed word processing typing and editing with accuracy and speed.
- Coordinated marketing strategies for in-house advertising, promotions and sales.
- Demonstrated strong phones skills, maintaining excellent customer relations.
- Hired, trained, supervised and scheduled staff members.

SANTA BARBARA COUNTY, (Medical Records Department)   1981-83
Medical Clerk/Computer Trainer
- Trained employees in data entry procedures on a new IBM computer system.
- Traveled daily to clinics, working closely with programmers, subcontractors, management and staff throughout the Santa Barbara county area.
- Typed and filed medical records; answered phones.

EDUCATION
Front Office Assistant Graduate
<u>Kellogg Business Institute</u>
Santa Barbara, CA, 1989

RACHEL C. FIELDING
3920 Remington Street
Ft. Collins, CO 80524
(303) 224-0094

OBJECTIVE
A Cancer Registrar position

CURRENT PROFESSIONAL EXPERIENCE

PORTER MEMORIAL HOSPITAL, DENVER, CO   1988-present
Cancer Registrar
- Plan, administer and direct the operation of the Cancer Registry.
- Assemble and disseminate Cancer Registry data collected on a daily basis.
- Obtain and abstract diagnoses, procedures, extent of cancer disease from patient medical records on a daily basis.
- Code daily topography/morphology of tumor cases using ICD-9-CM/ICD-0 systems.
- Maintain confidentiality and security of patient data stored in the Cancer Registry.
- Obtain end results on quality of life and length of survival from all living patients.
- Identify, organize and maintain a daily data system of all reportable cancer cases in the hospital.
- Coordinate the activities of the Cancer Registry with the Cancer Committee, Tumor Board and Tumor Conference.
- Develop and maintain quality control of case finding, abstracting, coding, follow-up and data processing procedures.
- Prepare narrative reports and graphic presentations of data design, tables, charts and graphs.
- Monitor coding integrity for ICD-9-CM and CPT classification systems.
- Coordinate activities with medical records, radiology, pathology and outpatient services.

EDUCATION
Registered Records Administrator, 1984
Regis College, Denver, CO

Certified Medical Assistant, 1979
Medical Careers Training Center, Ft. Collins, CO

PREVIOUS EMPLOYMENT HISTORY
Quality Assurance Assistant, Poudre Valley Hospital, Ft. Collins, CO   1986-88
Medical Records Clerk, University Hospital, Denver, CO   1984-86
Medical Assistant, Ft. Collins Youth Clinic, Ft. Collins, CO   1979-84

RENEE ANNE BURNS
PO Box 4567
Ft. Collins, CO 80522
(303) 224-0000

Objective: A Clinical Affairs Coordinator position

PROFESSIONAL EXPERIENCE

Domestic Medical Device Regulatory Experience
- Prepare new product submittals to file with the FDA.
  - Write and coordinate Investigational Device Exemption (IDE) submissions.
- Coordinate and monitor clinical investigations.
- Develop and coordinate 510(k) submissions.
- Edit and coordinate product data sheet and literature projects.
- Provide regulatory support to product development/marketing personnel.

International Medical Device Experience
- Coordinate communications with international distributors to ensure international regulatory compliance. Knowledge of 1992 EEC ramifications.
- Prepare export approval requests for investigational devices.
- Introduced 56 catalog and special product devices to the Canadian market via Device Notifications and Notice of Compliance documents.
- Coordinate document translations as required by government regulations.

Special Skills
Technical Writing...GMP Compliance...Quality Assurance...Internal Auditing...Computer Literacy...Vascular Device Research...Scanning Electron...Microscopy...Laboratory Analysis...Training...Calibration...Inventory Control...Audio-Visual Materials...Direct Mail Marketing...Equipment Maintenance & Repair...Troubleshooting.

EDUCATION

AS Degree, Veterinary Technology
Texas State Technical Institute
Graduated w/honors: 1977, GPA: 3.8

EMPLOYMENT HISTORY

Regulatory Affairs Coordinator, Medical Services, Inc.,	1988-present
Quality Assurance Analyst, Medical Research Corp., Austin, TX	1982-88
Surgical Nurse/Histo-SEM Lab Tech, KMM & Assoc, Austin, TX	1979-82

TERI S. TURNER
2019 Rachel Court
Denver, CO 80210
(303) 778-0032

OBJECTIVE
A Home Care Patient Coordinator position

CURRENT PROFESSIONAL EXPERIENCE

HUMANA HOSPITAL, Denver, CO   1983-present
Home Care Patient Coordinator
- Attend discharge weekly rounds on the surgical orthopedic and neurology units.

- Discuss daily rounds with dietary nurses, social worker, doctors, physical therapist for potential discharges that may need home care.

- Contact patient and family regarding home care needs such as physical therapy, occupational therapy, registered nursing aide, social worker and equipment needs.

- Refer to outside agencies for suppliers of equipment, additional aide and housekeeping services.

- Meet with primary home care person to discuss patient needs and plans for home care.

- Refer to other home care agencies if hospital is unable to cover patient needs or by patient's request.

- Contact insurance companies to establish coverage for home care.

- Discuss with family appropriateness of patient discharge to home environment to determine if patient will be safe in that setting.

- Contact other agencies to help fund patient care when there is no insurance.

- Fill out forms with database and copy pertinent information from charts.

- Prepare coding for Medicare and third party pages from coding books.

- Present the functions of the home care agency services through the hospital to all interested persons, i.e., patients, family, doctor, friends and neighbors.

EDUCATION
BS Degree, Nursing, 1983
University of Northern Colorado, Greeley, CO

VERONICA (RONNIE) LINCOLN
3982 Holiday Road
Ft. Collins, CO 80526
(303) 226-0039

OBJECTIVE
A Volunteer Services Coordinator position at a hospital

CURRENT PROFESSIONAL EXPERIENCE

COORDINATOR OF JUNIOR VOLUNTEER SERVICES   1986-present
Poudre Valley Hospital, Ft. Collins, CO
* Coordinate services and supervise 100 young adults who volunteer in 20 departments for an average of 500 hours per month.
  -Recruit -screen -interview -train -schedule
* Teach business and human relation skills to teens.
* Process data management for 375+ volunteers.
* Present orientations for an average of 350 parents per year.
* Assess hospital needs for Junior Volunteer Services through surveys with department heads.
* Coordinate and lead tours; assist in recruitment and training of guides.
* Organize special hospital projects and activities for junior volunteers.
* Communicate and maintain close contact with department heads and staff who work with junior volunteer services.
* Serve as trustee for a scholarship trust fund.
* Participate in numerous professional State organizations.
* Help support and interpret departmental goals and the roles they play in to staff, volunteers, and the community.
* Perform secretarial responsibilities for the Department of Volunteer Services.

EDUCATION
BA Degree, Education, 1976
University of Colorado
Boulder, CO

AA Degree, Social and Behavior Science, 1972
Front Range Community College
Westminister, CO

PREVIOUS EMPLOYMENT HISTORY
Coordinator/Educator, Denver General Hospital, Denver, CO   1982-86
Educator, University Hospital, Denver, CO   1979-82
Program Coordinator, Colorado State University, Ft. Collins, CO   1976-79

DONNA P. PALASKY
8906 Taft Hill Road
Ft. Collins, CO 80526
(303) 226-0054

OBJECTIVE
A Dental Assistant position

PROFESSIONAL EXPERIENCE

Chairside Dental Experience
- Prepare patient for treatment and obtain dental records for dentist; make patient as comfortable as possible.
- Hand dentist the proper instruments and materials and keep the patient's mouth dry and clear by using suction devices.
- Sterilize and disinfect instruments and equipment.
- Prepare tray setups for dental procedures.
- Provide postoperative instruction to the patient; instruct patients in oral health care and preventive dentistry measures.
- Remove sutures, apply anesthetic and caries-preventive agents to the teeth and oral tissue, remove excess cement used in the filling process, and place rubber dams on the teeth to isolate them for individual treatment.

Dental Office Experience
- Greet patients; arrange and confirm appointments.
- Maintain accurate treatment records, send out bills, receive payments.
- Order dental supplies and materials.

Dental Laboratory Experience
- Prepare materials for making impressions and restorations, expose radiographs, and process dental X-ray film as directed by the dentist.
- Make casts of the teeth and mouth from impressions taken by the dentist.

EDUCATION
Certified Dental Assistant, 1982
Front Range Community College
Ft. Collins, CO

EMPLOYMENT HISTORY

Dental Assistant, Ft. Collins Dentistry, Ft. Collins, CO	1987-present
Dental Assistant, Front Range Dental Clinic, Ft. Collins, CO	1985-87
Dental Assistant, Stuart Smith, DDS, Fresno, CA	1982-85

CARA MARIA LUCCI
1100 Mead Court
Ft. Collins, CO 80526
(303) 226-8709

OBJECTIVE
A Dental Hygienist position

CURRENT PROFESSIONAL EXPERIENCE

DENTAL HYGIENIST   1986-present
Michael Shannon, DDS, Loveland, CO

- Provide preventive dental care and encourage patients to develop good oral hygiene skills.

- Evaluate patient's dental health.

- Clean and scale patients' teeth; remove calculus, stain, and plaque from above and below the gumline.

- Apply caries-preventive agents such as fluorides and pit and fissure sealants.

- Educate patients on plaque control; show patients how to select toothbrushes and use floss threaders.

- Expose and develop dental X-rays; place temporary fillings and periodontal dressings; remove sutures; polish and recontour amalgam restorations.

- Administer local anesthetics and nitrous oxide/oxygen analgesia; place and carve filling materials.

- Developed a successful communitywide dental health program.

EDUCATION
Bachelor's Degree, Dental Hygienist, 1975
UC School of Dentistry, Denver, CO

AFFILIATION
Member, American Dental Hygienists Assn.

PREVIOUS EMPLOYMENT HISTORY
Home Management, Travel, Study, Denver, CO	1982-86
Dental Hygienist, Jefferson County Health Care Svs., Denver, CO	1979-82
Dental Hygienist, Susan Jefferson, DDS, Denver, CO	1975-79

SHELLEY R. JENSEN
555 Park Avenue
Los Angeles, CA 90067
(213) 390-2222

Objective: A Clinical Dietitian Specialist position

QUALIFICATION SUMMARY:
Seven years' experience as a clinical dietician demonstrating thorough knowledge in infant and adult nutrition. Maintain excellent organizational skills with outstanding patient care and employee relations.

PROFESSIONAL EXPERIENCE:

Clinical Experience
- Received extensive clinical experience in nutritional care for as many as 2500 patients on tube feeding and TPN.
- Conducted studies and developed a successful Nutrition Support Team, a multi-disciplinary group utilized to maintain proper product use for effective patient care.
- Became main resource person for health care facilities throughout southern California to troubleshoot and answer questions regarding proper use of foods and products.

Public Relations Experience
- Conducted several demonstrations to promote health care products and to educate physicians and nurses at hospitals and professional organizations throughout Los Angeles county.
- Attended all sales demonstrations and worked closely with sales representatives to purchase products with the highest quality, and most appropriate and consistent for patient use.

EMPLOYMENT HISTORY:

Clinical Dietitian Specialist, General Hospital
Los Angeles, CA, 1984-present

Clinical Dietitian, Brotman Medical Center
Culver City, CA, 1980-84

EDUCATION:
- **BA Degree, Foods & Nutrition,** June 1979
  California State University at Northridge, cum laude
- **Certified Nutrition Support Dietician**

AFFILIATION:
Member, American Dietetic Association, No. R 512344

JENNIFER R. FOLEY
1102 Smith Street
Denver, CO 80210
(303) 778-9483

OBJECTIVE
A Clinical Dietitian position

PROFESSIONAL EXPERIENCE

Clinical Dietitian
- Provide nutritional services for critically ill, diabetic or obese patients in hospitals, nursing homes and clinics.
- Assess patients' nutritional needs, develop and implement nutrition programs, and evaluate and report the results.
- Confer with doctors and other health care professionals about each patient to coordinate nutritional intake with other treatments—medications in particular.
- Oversee the preparation of custom-mixed, high-nutrition formulas for patients requiring tube or intravenous feedings.
- Establish long-term nutritional care programs and a close monitoring system for diabetic patients.
- Ran the food service department and managed other dietitians for a nursing home.

Community Dietitian
- Counsel individuals and groups on topics from weight control to menu planning for diabetics.
- Conduct seminars at Colorado State University and University of Northern Colorado on nutritional practices designed to prevent disease and to promote good health.
- Evaluate individual needs, establish nutritional care plans, and communicate the principles of good nutrition in a way individuals and their families can understand.
- Collaborate with HMO staff in conducting educational sessions on alcoholism, smoking and hypertension.

Management Dietitian
- Plan and prepare large-scale meals for a hospital and nursing home.
- Supervise the planning, preparation and service of meals.
- Select, train, and direct other dietitians and food service supervisors and workers.
- Budget for and purchase food, equipment, and supplies.
- Enforce sanitary and safety regulations; prepare records and reports.
- Direct the dietetic department with a multimillion dollar budget; determine department policy; coordinate dietetic services with activities of other departments.

- More -

EDUCATION
BS, Food Science and Nutrition, 1979
Colorado State University
Ft. Collins, CO

Registered Dietitian
American Dietetic Association

PREVIOUS EMPLOYMENT HISTORY
Clinical/Management Dietitian, Denver General Hospital, Denver, CO   1986-present
Clinical Dietitian, North Colorado Medical Center, Greeley, CO   1883-86
Community Dietitian, Larimer County Health Dept., Ft. Collins, CO   1980-83
Clinical Dietitian, Columbine Care Center West, Ft. Collins, CO   1979-80

JENNIFER C. LAKE
4448 El Colegio #12
Goleta, CA 93117
(805) 968-3333

OBJECTIVE
An Internship as a Dietitian's Aide in a hospital

EDUCATION
BA Degree - Food & Nutrition
University of California, Santa Barbara
Graduation: 1994

RELATED COURSES
Nutrition, Institution Management, Psychology
Chemistry, Physiology, Sociology, Economics

RELATED EXPERIENCE

PEER HEALTH EDUCATOR   1992-present
UCSB Student Health Center, Santa Barbara, CA
- Counsel individuals and groups of students with all types of nutritional problems.
- Discuss deficiencies in the students' diet and effective ways of improvement.
- Conducted demonstrations to large groups of people on the following topics: *Dorm Food Survival, Eating for Athletes, Fat and Cholesterol.*
- Lead the nutrition group while serving as the Peer Health Coordinator.
- Developed public speaking skills that demonstrate confidence and poise.

STORE MANAGER   1990-91
Grandma Gerties Sandwich Shop, Goleta, CA
- Developed advertising that focused on a more diet conscious menu items.
- Created new menu items.
- Baked foods; learned to bake in large quantities.
- Interacted with customers daily, maintained excellent relations.
- Solved potential interpersonal problems among employees.
- Maintained opening and closing the store.

PREVIOUS EMPLOYMENT HISTORY
Sales Associate, Robinson's, Los Angeles, CA   1987-90
Grocery Clerk, Safeway Marketplace, Ft. Collins, CO   1985-87

JACQUELINE S. SWEENEY
3920 Gunther Road
Denver, CO 80210
(303) 778-0034

OBJECTIVE
Director of Volunteer Services

CURRENT PROFESSIONAL EXPERIENCE
PORTER MEMORIAL HOSPITAL, Denver, CO   1982-present
Director of Volunteer Services

- Coordinate activities of 375 + volunteers for all hospital departments.

- Orient, interview and place matriculating volunteer workers.

- Decide appropriateness of potential volunteers.

- Receive and evaluate job requests for volunteers from all departments.

- Supervise junior volunteer coordinator and clerk.

- Schedule volunteers in each service with volunteer chairman or supervisor.

- Coordinate volunteers and ER staff involved in Lifeline system.

- Conduct Lifeline pre-installation visits.

- Serve on committees and attend department managers meetings including the Auxiliary board meetings.

- Arrange meetings with each volunteer inservice group on a regular basis.

- Assist production of Auxiliary volunteers newsletter at least four times a year.

- Arrange and organize annual retreat for Auxiliary Board of Directors.

- Organize ongoing, special recognition of volunteers.

EDUCATION
MA Degree, Education, 1976
University of Colorado, Boulder, CO

PREVIOUS EMPLOYMENT HISTORY
Coordinator, Volunteer Svs., Porter Memorial Hospital, Denver, CO   1978-82
Program Coordinator, University of Colorado, Boulder, CO   1976-78

LINDSEY S. POZZER
1120 Stuart Street
Denver, CO 80262
(303) 270-0032

OBJECTIVE
Director of Clinical Home Care Services

CURRENT PROFESSIONAL EXPERIENCE

DENVER GENERAL HOSPITAL, Denver, CO   1981-present
Director of Clinical Home Care Services

- Coordinate patient care assignments to all professional staff and ensure timely, and when needed, emergency response.

- Respond to community calls for department information; assess and recommend assistance for sick patients at home.

- Serve as clinical resource person, providing appropriate office management support and liaison for staff to physicians, community agencies and families.

- Review Medicare records prior to claim submission for appropriateness of staff documentation.

- Ensure clinical care is in compliance with Medicare, State rules and regulations.

- Maintain and monitor professional competency growth of staff and self.

- Participate on selected committees to represent and integrate home care services.

- Review and monitor work with staff to meet productivity and provide budget input.

- Develop new and needed policies and procedures for patient care and staff duties.

EDUCATION
BS Degree, Nursing, 1975
University of Colorado School of Nursing
Grand Junction, CO

PREVIOUS EMPLOYMENT HISTORY
Home Care Coordinator, University Hospital, Denver, CO   1978-81
Staff Nurse, University Hospital, Denver, CO   1975-78

MARIANNE LEESA TANDY
3947 Howes Street
Ft. Collins, CO 80522
(303) 223-9876

OBJECTIVE
A Maternal Child Education Services Coordinator position

CURRENT PROFESSIONAL EXPERIENCE

EDUCATION SERVICES COORDINATOR   1981-present
Poudre Valley Hospital, Ft. Collins, CO
- Evaluate and approve the maternal-child educational programs curriculum for the Ft. Collins community.

- Serve as resource person for the program instructors, providing guidance and instruction.

- Conduct a needs analysis of the community for the development of new maternal child educational programs.

- Develop new maternal child education programs as the need is validated.

- Select and evaluate instructors for the maternal-child education classes.

- Establish and maintain a collaborative relationship with the medical, nursing staff and community childbirth educators.

- Serve as a professional educator; teach classes, seminars, programs and presentations to the community at large.

- Evaluate audiovisual materials used for the programs and preview new materials.

- Develop, maintain, and market all printed promotional materials for the programs.

EDUCATION
MA Degree, Education, 1975
University of Colorado, Boulder, CO

BS Degree, Nursing, 1971
University of Colorado, Boulder, CO

PREVIOUS EMPLOYMENT HISTORY
Educator, University Hospital, Denver, CO   1975-81
Staff Nurse, Denver General Hospital, Denver, CO   1971-75

RUTH S. SIMON
1236 Marsden Drive
Denver, CO 80218
(303) 893-0034

OBJECTIVE
A Critical Care Nursing Educator position

CURRENT PROFESSIONAL EXPERIENCE

EDUCATOR OF CRITICAL CARE NURSING   1984-present
Denver General Hospital, Denver, CO
- Plan, develop, implement and evaluate nursing orientation program.
- Instruct CPR, ACLS, EKG, and physical assessment classes necessary for hospital RN's, paramedics, EKG technician employees and the community.
- Coordinate and instruct regional training program for ICU nurses four times a year.
- Serve as education liaison for nurses; coordinate all inservice programs for ICCU, IV team, ASAP, and PACU units.
- Orient hospital and community members to ACTRONIC, CPR, EKG and ACLS programs.
- Instruct team in critical care nursing concepts, patient care, invasive monitoring, operation of therapeutic technology, critical decision making, patient safety and collaboration with medical staff.
- Develop, implement/evaluate competency testing skills program in critical care.
- Serve as resource person for hospital and community nurses that may require immediate action or advice about patient care problems; involves notification at home, in the evening, nights and weekends.
- Research latest methods, instrumentation and techniques and incorporate it into instruction, nursing care and policy and procedures.
- Serve as a role model and provide career counseling for hospital nurses, community members, student nurses and other hospital personnel.
- Member of the quality assurance committee for units responsible for any education oriented action and ongoing assessment of problems.
- Serve as a member of NEAC primary nursing collaborative practice, ICCU medical, nursing unit staff and education meeting.

EDUCATION
MA Degree, Education, 1984
University of Colorado, Boulder, CO

BS Degree, Nursing, 1979
University of Northern Colorado, Greeley, CO

Critical Care Nursing Certificate
West Valley College, Saratoga, CA

JOANNE LESLIE BORDOFSKY
2901 Lake Street
Colorado Springs, CO 80909
(719) 475-0023

OBJECTIVE
A Nurse Educator position

CURRENT PROFESSIONAL EXPERIENCE
NURSE EDUCATOR   1984-present
Memorial Hospital, Colorado Springs, CO

- Serve as educational liaison for orthopedic, neurology and rehabilitation units.
- Educate staff in assessing, learning needs and facilitating educational programs to identify/research quality assurance problems and develop policy and procedures.
- Assess, treat, teach and evaluate in- and out-patients with specific learning needs.
- Serve as clinical consultant to nursing staff and physicians to evaluate patient care and to problem solve specific patient care issues.
- Coordinate, supervise and evaluate educational experiences for orientees on orthopedics, neurology and rehabilitation units.
- Assess, design and evaluate patient education materials, programs and brochures.
- Evaluate and coordinate the Acute Neurology and Arthritis Interdisciplinary Teams; initiate and facilitate multidisciplinary patient staffing and family conferences.
- Collaborate with Head Nurses on Ortho, Neuro, and Rehab Units to establish goals, evaluate patient care, plan educational programs and provide professional support.
- Assess learning needs of nursing staff and ancillary personnel; respond to needs by initiating experiences, providing one-on-one instruction and educational programs.
- Serve as community resource person and consultant to provide health information relating to wellness and specific diseases; to identify support groups and to facilitate referral to community agencies.
- Plan, coordinate, teach and evaluate workshops, seminars and classes for hospital employees, local and national professional nursing organizations.
- Serve as role model for nursing, by maintaining a professional image, involvement in professional organizations, keeping abreast of current nursing and education issues and maintaining expertise in specialty areas.
- Act as resource person and consultant, representing the Education Department in designated nursing and hospital committees.

HOSPITAL COMMITTEE CONSULTANT
Nursing Personnel Council
Eldercare Task Force
Rehab Planning Committee
Acute Neuro Team Member
Nursing Education Advisory Committee
Quality Assurance Committee

- More -

EDUCATION
MA Degree, Education, 1979
University of California, Los Angeles

BS Degree, Nursing, 1974
University of Northern Colorado, Greeley, CO

PREVIOUS EMPLOYMENT HISTORY
Nurse Educator, UC Medical Center, Westwood, CA   1979-84
Staff Nurse, St. Joseph Hospital, Denver, CO   1976-79
Staff Nurse, Spalding Rehabilitation Hospital, Denver, CO   1974-76

LINDY R. ROLLINS
1837 Oak Street
Greeley, CO 80631
(303) 421-0021

OBJECTIVE
A Nurse Educator position

CURRENT PROFESSIONAL EXPERIENCE

GREELEY MEMORIAL HOSPITAL, Greeley, CO   1987-present
Nurse Educator/Counselor
- Instruct and counsel out-patients in the areas of breast cancer, benign breast disease, mammography and BSE.
- Develop breast-related educational programs for community groups and health care providers in the Radiology Department.
- Research current medical and nursing literature and compile reference material.
- Collaborate with Director of Radiology in arranging for meeting places, publicity and scheduling of Breast Diagnostic Center (BDC) programs.
- Develop and update teaching aids, slide shows and table displays used for health fair and educational purposes.
- Assist Director of Radiology in follow-up of patients' concerns of BDC operation.
- Complete a history risk analysis form on each BDC patient.
- Perform a complete breast exam on patients and provide individual BSE instruction.
- Collect/compile pathology data on all patients having breast surgery at the hospital.
- Correlate and respond to inquiries by radio and newspaper media with information to promote the Breast Diagnostic Center.
- Correspond with American Cancer Society in ordering pamphlets, reporting use of their materials and in representing BDC on ACS committees.
- Monitor and maintain a functional filing system.

EDUCATION
BA Degree, Education, 1986
University of Colorado, Boulder, CO

AAS Degree, Nursing, 1982
Front Range Community College
Westminster, CO

PREVIOUS EMPLOYMENT HISTORY
Staff Nurse, Greeley Memorial Hospital, Greeley, CO   1985-87
Staff Nurse, Porter Memorial Hospital, Denver, CO   1984-85
Staff Nurse, Swedish Medical Center, Englewood, CO   1982-84

CHLOE T. TALBOTT
3210 Shields Avenue
Ft. Collins, CO 80524
(303) 221-0032

OBJECTIVE
A Senior EEG Technologist position

CURRENT PROFESSIONAL EXPERIENCE

EEG TECHNOLOGIST   1983-present
Poudre Valley Hospital, Ft. Collins, CO
- Perform EEG studies on patients with neurological problems to rule out the cause of brain damage, seizures, resulting from a stroke or head injury; microfilm EEGs.
- Set up patients, record and monitor surgery for Carotid Endarterectomy to make sure patient doesn't suffer a stroke; document any pertinent history.
- Perform evoked potential studies to rule out the early diagnosis of Multiple Sclerosis and brain tumors.
- Perform sleep studies for patients with Sleep Apnea.
- Schedule appointments for in- and out-patients receiving diagnostic procedures from the Neuroscience Lab.
- Maintain accurate records of completed tests.
- Transport hospital patients to and from the EEG lab or transport the machine to patient's bedside.
- Deliver patient test results to hospital or out-patient chart.
- Order supplies for the Neurology Department; clean and repair equipment.

EDUCATION
Registered EEG Technologist, 1983
St. John's Hospital
School of EEG Technology
Springfield, IL

AFFILIATION
Member, American Society of
Electroneurodiagnostic Technologists (ASET)

PROFESSIONAL PROFILE
- Ability to perform basic EEG proficiently with demonstrative knowledge of cortical depth recording procedures and electro cerebral silence recording.
- Recognize/understand EEG activity displayed; identify and correct artifacts.
- Work well with critically ill patients, young children and psychiatric patients.
- Outstanding ability to perform auditory, visual, and sensory evoked response studies.

BETTY LOU HYLAND
1412 Horsetooth Road
Ft. Collins, CO 80525
(303) 225-7777

Objective: A Cardiology Technician position

PROFESSIONAL EXPERIENCE

PORTER MEMORIAL HOSPITAL, Denver, CO   1986-present
EKG Technician
- Schedule patients and taxing case histories for a 350+ bed hospital.
- Assist nurse with pulmonary function tests, electroencephlograms and exercise studies.
- Work with specialists on metabolic studies and treadmill stress testing.
- Interpret EKG's and check Pacemaker.
- Help nurse with Pacemaker insertions, reprogramming, pericardiocentesis and emergency "code blue" situations.
- Scan holter monitors on highly sophisticated computer system.
- Maintain medical records and files.

UNIVERSITY HOSPITAL, Denver, CO   1982-86
Diagnostic Technician
- Scheduled patients for a 100 bed facility.
- Maintained accurate files of patients' medical records.
- Typed and transcribed patients' medical histories and handled phone calls and correspondence.
- Attended cardiology conferences.
- Ordered medical histories for the department.

DENVER RESEARCH CENTER, Aurora, CO   1979-82
Lab Technician
- Soldered and sterilized equipment and maintained quality assurance.
- Updated lab records.

EDUCATION

Certified EKG Techician, 1979
Emily Griffith Opportunity School
Denver, CO

KIM L. SONG
544 Peterson Drive
Ft. Collins, CO 80524
(303) 224-0043

OBJECTIVE
An EKG Technician position for a hospital

PROFESSIONAL EXPERIENCE

EKG TECHNICIAN
Poudre Valley Hospital, Ft. Collins, CO   1987-present

- Operate the electrocardiograph machine to help diagnose heart disease, monitor the effect of drug therapy and analyze changes in the condition of patient's heart.

- Record and prepare electrocardiograms for analysis at the hospital as well as private offices of the physician.

- Perform Holter monitoring, stress tests, venipuncture, phlebotomy, specimen collection, capillary punctures, blood cell determination, blood chemistry tests and urinalysis.

- Ability to quickly recognize and correct crossed leads, incorrect lead placement or electrical interference that may prevent an accurate reading.

- Schedule appointments, type interpretations, maintain patient's EKG files and care for equipment.

MEDICAL LABORATORY ASSISTANT
Swedish Medical Center, Englewood, CO   1985-87

- Assist EKG Technician with routine diagnostic procedures and heart patients in the cardiology department.

- Maintain patient EKG files, type interpretations and schedule appointments.

SPECIAL TRAINING
EKG Technician, 1985
Emily Griffith Opportunity School
Denver, CO

HANNA P. PHILLIPS
4567 Mathews Street
Ft. Collins, CO 80524
(303) 224-5554

OBJECTIVE
An Emergency Department Technician

CURRENT PROFESSIONAL EXPERIENCE
EMERGENCY DEPARTMENT TECHNICIAN   1988-present
Poudre Valley Hospital, Ft. Collins, CO
- Take patients' vital signs and medical history working under the charge nurse.

- Perform and chart initial patient assessment.

- Initiate or assist emergency team with CPR.

- Care for wounds and control hemorrhage aseptic techniques and dressings.

- Recognize signs/symptoms of impairment with injury to the central nervous system, medical emergencies, and complications; act accordingly.

- Educate patients/family with follow-up care and safety as directed by physician.

- Transport patient to and from emergency department, to other departments and patient floors in the hospital.

- Assist lab, X-ray, EKG, and other departments and floors when needed.

- Check department area for outdated supplies and stock working areas, maintaining a safe environment.

- Maintain the emergency department in a clean and orderly condition.

EDUCATION
AAS Degree, Nursing, 1986
Front Range Community College
Westminster, CO

Certified Firefighter, 1984
Hancock College, Santa Maria, CA

PREVIOUS EMPLOYMENT HISTORY
Staff Nurse, Hospice of Metro Denver, Denver, CO   1986-88
Firefighter, City of Denver, Denver, CO   1984-86

Emergency Medical Services Education Coordinator— Combination Resume

DONNA MARIE RIFTKIN
2859 Lory Park Drive
Ft. Collins, CO 80526
(303) 222-9958

OBJECTIVE
An Emergency Medical Services Education Coordinator position

CURRENT PROFESSIONAL EXPERIENCE
POUDRE VALLEY HOSPITAL, Ft. Collins, CO   1985-present
Emergency Medical Services Education Coordinator
- Coordinate educational programs for the hospital ambulance paramedics emergency department employees and pre-hospital emergency providers...
  -police -sheriff -search & rescue team -community organizations
- Contract instructors, schedule, process student applications and implement Emergency Medical Technician and CPR programs.
- Teach recertification and coordinate all educational materials.
- Contract multiple instructors for Advanced Cardiac Life Support programs.
  -Teach classes, process State certificates, counsel students, and provide materials.
- Teach, maintain records and coordinate continuing education for EMT Recertification to the Pre-hospital Quick Response Teams.
- Develop and author changes in County resolution as member of the Larimer County Emergency Services Committee.
- Developed and revised hospital Disaster Plan and EMS Orientation Policy and Procedure Manual. Supervise field exercises.
- Created policy, procedures and implementation of computerized learning system.
- Counsel prospective EMT students of paramedics on educational goals, and prospective employment opportunities.
- Serve as team member of Education Dept. staff for planning, developing, coordinating/implementing educational services for the hospital/community services:
  -Poison Talks -Proofing your Family -Ambulance demonstrations for Poudre R-1 School District, City of Ft. Collins and Larimer County.

EDUCATION
Certified Emergency Medical Technician
Poudre Valley Hospital, Ft. Collins, CO

Paramedics Training, 1979
St. Anthony's Hospital, Denver, CO

MA Degree, Education, 1985
University of Colorado, Boulder, CO

PREVIOUS EMPLOYMENT HISTORY
Paramedic, Denver General Hospital, Denver, CO   1979-85

LESLIE TAMARA GOULD
PO Box 1567
Santa Barbara, CA 93190
(805) 966-1111

Objective: Emergency Medical Technician

PROFESSIONAL HIGHLIGHTS

- Licensed Psychiatric Technician #LG 00000 since 1985.
- Certified in CPR, first aid, management of assaultive behavior.
- Ability to speak and understand sign language and Spanish.
- Team player with the ability to work independently.
- Attended communication and anger management workshops.
- Feel confident working in stressful, often unpredictable, potentially dangerous situations.

PROFESSIONAL EXPERIENCE

MOBILE CRISIS INTERVENTION SPECIALIST   1984-present
The Mobile Unit, LCSW, Inc, Santa Barbara, CA
- Mobile crisis team member.
 - Perform mental status exams. Determine suicide/homicide potential.
 - Help patients negotiate acute crises, forestall hospitalization, prevent recurrences.
 - Arrange inpatient psychiatric hospitalization as voluntary patient, or under W&I 5150 law as deemed necessary.

EMERGENCY MEDICAL TECHNICIAN   1982-84
Bay Ambulance, Morro Bay, CA
- Provided basic emergency medical services.
 - Taught CPR to law enforcement officers, firefighters, hospital personnel private citizens.

COUNSELING/TEACHING ASSISTANT   1980-82
Juvenile Services Center, (Detention Facility), San Luis Obispo, CA
- Assisted in all academic areas of the classroom.
 - Led communication groups and conducted monthly first aid classes.

EDUCATION
Certified Emergency Medical Technician, 1982
Swedish Medical Center, Englewood, CO

BA Degree, Psychology, 1979
University of California, Santa Barbara

AA Degree, Psychiatric Technology
Ventura College, Ventura, CA, 1975

PETER S. MAXWELL
2850 Robertson Street
Ft. Collins, CO 80524
(303) 224-9584

OBJECTIVE
An Environmental Health/Safety Manager position

CURRENT PROFESSIONAL EXPERIENCE

POUDRE VALLEY HOSPITAL, Ft. Collins, CO   1988-present
Environmental Health/Safety Manager
- Serve as permanent member of the hospital monthly Safety Inspection Team and Safety Committee.
- Keep administration informed on safety and health issues which present liabilities to the hospital.
- Anticipate, recognize, evaluate and control factors in the workplace which may cause injury, illness and inefficiency for staff, patients and visitors.
- Coordinate closely with Plant Services Director, Infection Control Coordinator, and Employee Health Director on topics related to safety and health.
- Investigate accidents and potential hazards and take necessary action.
- Serve as resource person for consultation to hospital staff and the community.
- Develop and monitor policies, procedures, and safeguards related to hazardous materials handling, working with all hospital departments.
- Coordinate with local state and federal agencies where appropriate.
- Established a Hazard Communication Standard program which involves proper labeling, storage and employee education related to hazardous materials.
- Maintain contact with universities, professional societies, and local industries to keep current on innovations in safety and health issues.

EDUCATION
MS Degree, Environmental Studies, 1979
University of California at Santa Barbara

BS Degree, Environmental Health, 1984
Colorado State University, Ft. Collins, CO

PREVIOUS EMPLOYMENT HISTORY
Public Health Environmentalist, Larimer County, Ft. Collins, CO   1979-88
Public Health Environmentalist, County of Ventura, Ventura, CA   1977-79

DAPHNE P. LYNDS
437 Fir Street
Denver, CO 80218
(303) 839-0001

OBJECTIVE
A part-time position as a Gastrointestinal Technician

CURRENT PROFESSIONAL EXPERIENCE
POUDRE VALLEY HOSPITAL, Ft. Collins, CO   1985-present
Certified Gastrointestinal Technician I

- Coordinate, assist and carry out GI procedures for in- and out-patients.

- Monitor patient status during and post procedure.

- Pass tubes, start/monitor IV's and give PO, IM, IV and SQ medication to patients.

- Set up and assist physicians with endoscopic procedures.

- Carry out monitor, esophageal, manometry under physician direction.

- Schedule procedures for the GI laboratory, X-ray, OR and follow up appointments with referring physicians.

- Arrange patients daily GI procedures working closely with all hospital floors.

- Communicate pre and post procedures to in-patients and to nursing personnel.

- Carry out immediate pre and post procedure care of out-patients and educate patients and their families.

- Clean, maintain and stock equipment, procedure rooms and carts; order supplies and medications.

- Log and chart all daily procedures and medications; record patient charges.

EDUCATION
Certified Nursing Program, 1980
Front Range Community College
Westminster, CO

PREVIOUS EMPLOYMENT HISTORY
Licensed Practical Nurse, Rose Medical Center, Denver, CO   1984-85
Licensed Practical Nurse, United Hospital, Longmont, CO   1982-84
Licensed Practical Nurse, University Hospital, Denver, CO   1980-82

SALLY S. WEEKS
5678 9th Street
Rock Springs, WY 82902
(307) 362-9985

OBJECTIVE
A Histology Technician position

CURRENT PROFESSIONAL EXPERIENCE

HISTOLOGY TECHNICIAN
Memorial Hospital of Sweetwater County, Rock Springs, WY   1989-present
- Prepare microscope slides of tissue and body fluids for detection of pathological conditions.

- Make up solutions.

- Perform special stain procedures.

- Store and appropriately dispose of tissue and body fluids.

- Log in specimens.

- Prepare patients' billing; keep monthly record of workload; order supplies; maintain files of blocks and slides.

- Keep work area clean; answer telephones.

EDUCATION
Histologist Technician Certification, 1989
Penrose-St. Francis Healthcare Systems
Colorado Springs, CO

Registered Histologist
American Society of Clinical Pathologists (ASCP)

Certified Medical Assistant, 1987
Medical Careers Training Center, Ft. Collins, CO

PREVIOUS EMPLOYMENT HISTORY
Assistant Lab Technician, General Hospital, Denver, CO   1987-89
Medical Assistant, Denver Medical Clinic, Denver, CO   1986-87

GEORGIA S. SAVOY
3461 Mathews Street
Denver, CO 80218
(303) 399-0002

OBJECTIVE
Home Care Supervisor of Clinical Services

CURRENT PROFESSIONAL EXPERIENCE

UNIVERSITY HOSPITAL, Denver, CO   1985-present
Home Care Supervisor of Clinical Services
- Hire, orient, train and supervise clinical staff in the management of patient care.
- Assess patient admissions for proper patient care.
- Assign staff to case load based on qualifications of staff and geographical location.
- Establish and maintain a system for documentation review for clinical progress notes to insure compliance with Medicare regulations for reimbursement.
- Conduct regular patient care conferences for multi-disciplinary coordination of care, case finding, and case management.
- Identify areas of need for education of staff and implement an educational plan for individuals as well as the agency and clinical staff as a whole.
- Evaluate quality assurance activities; developed an ongoing QA program identifying problems with follow through to enhance improved quality of care.
- Maintain clinical records meeting legal JCAHO/Medicare regulatory requirements.
- Develop patient care policies and procedures that provide for continuity of care.

PROFESSIONAL PROFILE
- Special ability to assess patient's needs for home care and interpret to hospital staff and physicians the appropriateness and need for home care services.
- Excellent interpersonal skills and ability to provide leadership and direction to staff and enhance team building.
- Outstanding ability to work with special contract services as well as with the public to market services.
- Gained thorough knowledge of Medicare home health regulations for skilled care and reimbursement.
- Demonstrate leadership ability, integrity and managerial/supervisory skills.

EDUCATION
BS Degree, Nursing, 1984
University of Northern Colorado, Greeley, CO

PREVIOUS EMPLOYMENT HISTORY
Home Care Coordinator, UC Medical Center, Denver, CO   1983-85
Home Care Assistant, Denver General Hospital, Denver, CO   1981-83

FRANKLYN SAMSON FORRESTER
1234 East Road
Goleta, CA 93117
(805) 964-1111

Objective: Hospital Administrator

PROFESSIONAL PROFILE
- Served as executive with successful leadership pattern since 1960.
- Maintained achievements in retirement campus administration, management and operations; corporate and business development.
- Developed effective fiscal operations, funding program, staff and leadership.
- Major marketing objectives achieved for national and local programs.

PROFESSIONAL EXPERIENCE
Strategic Planning
- Served as Campus Administrator during $15M rebuilding program for 16-acre campus from 1982-90.
- Initiated the development of retirement facility - Modesto, CA, 1967-68.
- Assisted in acquisition of major hospital for Eskaton.
- Established long range plans for Samarkand-Annual Updates.
- Developed three regional offices for Corporate Planning Association.

Operations
- Eight consecutive years of meeting corporate fiscal objectives while completing rebuilding program 1982-90. Operations budget is $6.5 million 1990.
- Strong resident relations contributing to a positive program, major gifts and resident satisfaction.
- Received awards five consecutive years for reducing Workmen's Compensation claims resulting in $30-40K a year in savings.
- Established excellent food and environmental services and marketing program.
- Established operational policies and procedures for campus - each department, performance standards for each employee position.
- President, Director and CEO of two proprietary operations:
Corporate Planning Associates and Mastercarve Products, Inc.

Development Program
- Directed capital campaigns for local and regional church $300K to $2.5M.
- Board of Directors for Board of Finance of Christian Church (National).
- Capital campaign Director - Eskaton American River Hospital.
- Established Samarkand Long Range Development Program.
- Expanded Good Neighbor and Free Care Endowment Funds by $500K at Samarkand.

- More -

PROFESSIONAL EXPERIENCE (Continued)

Marketing Program
- Directed marketing program for Eskaton Corporation Data Processing, Facility Acquisition, Human Resource Services and Waste Management Systems...Local - Statewide - Nationally.
- Developed successful marketing program for Samarkand Retirement Campus leading to consistent occupancy level.

EDUCATION

Masters, Business Administration
Golden Gate University, Sacramento, California
1982-in progress

Masters, Phillips University, Enid, Oklahoma
Graduate Seminary, 1958

Bachelor's Degree, Chapman College
Orange, California, 1954

AFFILIATIONS

Board of Directors: (Partial)
California Association of Homes for the Aging
Pacific School of Religion - Berkeley
Chapman College - Orange
Corporate Planning Associates, Inc.
Rotary Club, Santa Barbara
Transition House - Santa Barbara
Love Yourself Foundation - Santa Barbara
Visiting Nurses Association - Modesto
YMCA - Modesto
Oklahoma Association of Christian Churches

EMPLOYMENT HISTORY

Campus Administrator, Samarkand of Santa Barbara, CA	1982-90
Administrator, Marketing Director, Eskaton Hospital, Sacramento, CA	1976-82
CEO Corporate & Business Development, Sacramento, CA	1972-76
Director of Development and Community Relations Eskaton, Sacramento, CA	1970-72

DAWN ELLEN PRAIRIE
3854 Wood Street
Ft. Collins, CO 80521
(303) 221-0002

OBJECTIVE
Hospital Fitness Coordinator

CURRENT PROFESSIONAL EXPERIENCE

POUDRE VALLEY HOSPITAL, Ft. Collins, CO   1979-present
Fitness Coordinator (Healthaware Program)
- Develop and provide fitness programs to the hospital employees and community members which are an integral part of the whole wellness program.
- Hire, evaluate, educate, schedule and supervise fitness instructors.
- Develop and monitor class formats for normal and special populations providing new programs that increase revenues and appeal to a wider range of participants.
- Provide monthly evaluations and inservices for fitness instructors.
- Wrote and continue to update the existing educational manual.
- Market new programs through public speaking presentations, telemarketing and personal contacts.
- Interface with other instructors of weight loss and diabetes exercise classes.
- Register member and collect monies due.
- Provide one-on-one fitness evaluations and special monthly educational programs for participants and community members.
- Teach fitness classes when regular instructors are absent.
- Design and implement evaluation procedures for classes.
- Maintain budget for entire program.

EDUCATION
BS Degree, Exercise & Sports Medicine, 1979
Colorado State University
Ft. Collins, CO

Certified Aerobics Instructor
Certified Choreography & Low Impact Aerobics
Aerobic Fitness Association of American

PREVIOUS EMPLOYMENT HISTORY
Aerobics Instructor, Ft. Collins Health Club, Ft. Collins, CO   1977-79
Aerobics Instructor, Fitness Plus, Ft. Collins, CO   1975-77
Aerobics Instructor, Healthworks, Ft. Collins, CO   1973-75

LANDER P. SHORT
1287 Maple Street
Ft. Collins, CO 80524
(303) 224-5021

OBJECTIVE
An Infection Control Coordinator position

CURRENT PROFESSIONAL EXPERIENCE

POUDRE VALLEY HOSPITAL, Ft. Collins, CO   1985-present
Infection Control Coordinator

- Participate with Infection Control Committee to interpret and manage infection.

- Serve as liaison between hospital and the Infection Control Committee.

- Assist in developing and implementing improved prevention, detection and control.

- Implement protocol in regards to management of staff exposure to communicate any infectious disease.

- Ensure reporting of all disease to the local and State Health Department.

- Cooperate in the surveillance study with the Centers for Disease Control.

- Coordinate infection control programs working closely with head nurses, department heads and administration.

- Orient all employees with regard to infection control.

- Coordinate and implement daily isolation and barrier precautions.

- Ascertain efficiency of hospital sterilization and disinfection methods.

- Monitor all areas of hospital for sanitation problems and consult/advise to resolve.

- Make daily rounds on all nursing service and support services.

EDUCATION
BS Degree, Microbiology, 1977
Colorado State University, Ft. Collins, CO

PREVIOUS EMPLOYMENT HISTORY
Infection Control Assistant, General Hospital, Los Angeles, CA   1979-85
Research Lab Assistant, UC Medical Center, Denver, CO   1977-79

HARRY STUART WILSON
432 Epic Park Drive
Ft. Collins, CO 80525
(303) 225-0003

OBJECTIVE
A Laboratory Assistant position

PROFESSIONAL EXPERIENCE
COLORADO STATE UNIVERSITY, Ft. Collins, CO   1989-present
<u>Laboratory Assistant I</u>
- Assist technicians in preparing for and running routine tests and analyses on food, soils, water, air plants, body fluids, and tissue.
- Clean and sterilize laboratory equipment, work space and laboratory area.
- Prepare and label media, solutions, dyes and stains.
- Assist in collecting, processing and preparing samples; grow tissue cultures.
- Keep laboratory records and notes including related laboratory clerical work.
- Assemble kits for laboratory examinations.
- Assist in maintaining laboratory supplies and equipment.
- Assist technician in supervising and training other laboratory volunteer staff.

UNIVERSITY OF COLORADO, Boulder, CO   1986-89
<u>Laboratory Assistant I</u>
- Clean/sterilize slides, pipettes, test tubes, petri dishes, flasks and rubber tubing.
- Operate autoclave, sterilizers and ovens; clean and dust laboratory furniture.
- Make routine and simple examinations under close supervision.
- Assist technicians by procuring ingredients and distributing and storing media; help make simple solution and distilled water.
- Assemble simple kits for laboratory examinations.
- Deliver supplies and equipment.
- Bottle solutions; sharpen, clean, and sterilize surgical instruments.
- Prepare routine slides under close supervision and draw blood.

PROFESSIONAL PROFILE
- Gained skills in laboratory techniques, terminology and equipment.
- Follow written and oral instruction with attention to detail while performing laboratory tests.
- Ability to assist, direct, and supervise other employees.
- Exercise care in handling, cleaning, and sterilizing laboratory glassware and equipment.
- Developed excellent manual dexterity for laboratory performance.

EDUCATION
Certified Medical Lab Technician, 1985-86
<u>T.H. Pickens Tech Center</u>, Aurora, CO

JONAH DAVID EDMUNDTON
1234 Garfield Street
Ft. Collins, CO 80524
(303) 224-5540

OBJECTIVE
A Laboratory Assistant Supervisor

PROFESSIONAL EXPERIENCE

LABORATORY ASSISTANT SUPERVISOR   1987-present
CSU Student Health Center
- Supervise laboratory assistants in performing maintenance, preparation of media, specimens, and routine analysis.
- Participate and supervise receiving, checking and numbering laboratory specimens.
- Supervise the preparation of specimen collection packages.
- Instruct lower-level assistants in the use of autoclaves, automatic pipettes, sterilizers, balances and PH meter.
- Maintain records and reports of all activities performed.

LABORATORY ASSISTANT II
- Assist professional laboratory personnel in performing examination of blood, spinal fluid, water and dairy products.
- Inoculate prescribed media with water, milk and biological samples being examined.
- Prepare a wide variety of culture media solutions and other standardized recipes.
- Participate in simple laboratory tests.
- Maintain laboratory equipment, supplies and inventory control.
- Keep a supply of culture media available for the laboratory staff.
- Maintain records and reports of all activities performed.

PROFESSIONAL PROFILE
- Ability to assign and supervise work diplomatically.
- Gained thorough knowledge of basic laboratory principles, techniques, terminology and equipment.
- Knowledge of basic principles of physical and biologic sciences.
- Instruct students with use and maintenance of laboratory equipment.
- Follow written and oral instructions with attention to detail.
- Exercise care in handling, cleaning, and sterilizing laboratory glassware and equipment while performing laboratory tests.
- Maintain good manual dexterity for the performance of laboratory duties.

EDUCATION
AAS Degree, Medical Lab Technologist, 1987
Arapahoe Community College
Littleton, CO

HELEN PAULINE LILLIAN
234 Wood Street
Ft. Collins, CO 80521
(303) 221-2223

OBJECTIVE
A Laboratory Coordinator position

PROFESSIONAL EXPERIENCE
COLORADO STATE UNIVERSITY   1989-present
Laboratory Coordinator I

- Schedule and supervise laboratory assistants, students, part-time and work study personnel in proper use of equipment.

- Wash glassware, instruments and prepare media, solutions and other materials.

- Consult with faculty, staff and students to provide supportive service in research, teaching and special projects.

- Maintain storage areas and dispense materials.

- Assist department head with budget preparation.

- Establish supply levels, purchase supplies and maintain inventory control.

- Perform technical work to prepare laboratories for classes and assist with studies involving use of equipment.

- Keep accurate records and prepare reports.

PROFESSIONAL PROFILE
- Gained considerable knowledge of standard laboratory instruments, equipment and techniques of testing.

- Supervise staff with diplomacy and tact.

- Coordinate use of laboratory facilities in a highly efficient manner.

- Skilled in using standard laboratory instruments and equipment.

EDUCATION
AAS Degree, Medical Lab Technologist, 1988
Arapahoe Community College
Littleton, Colorado

HARRISON S. MANNING
112 Buckeye Street
Ft. Collins, CO 80524
(303) 224-5880

OBJECTIVE
A Laboratory Technician position

PROFESSIONAL EXPERIENCE

UNIVERSITY OF NORTHERN COLORADO, Greeley, CO   1988-present
Laboratory Technician I
- Prepare a wide variety of culture media from standardized recipes.
- Plate inoculum and stain cultures according to standard procedures and make routine plate counts.
- Take blood samples from laboratory animals or human patients by cardiac or venous and capillary punctures.
- Prepare and sterilize surgical instruments and linen packs for animal surgery.
- Perform routine histological procedures including cutting, embedding, staining, coverslipping and labeling.
- Clean and maintain laboratory and work area; disassemble, clean, sterilize, and reassemble organ perfusion chambers.
- Repair laboratory equipment.
- Prepare reports and keep records of tests, analyses and results.

PROFESSIONAL PROFILE

- Gained considerable knowledge of materials, techniques, and procedures of a variety of standardized laboratory tests.
- Technical knowledge of the biological and physical sciences applied to laboratory assignments.
- Ability to perform a variety of routine laboratory tests and analysis.
- Follow specific procedures and observe and record results accurately.
- Ability to establish and maintain effective working relationships with others.
- Skilled in the use of standard laboratory instruments, equipment and manipulative techniques.

EDUCATION

Certified Medical Lab Technician, 1985
T.H. Pickens Tech Center, Aurora, CO

JORGE LEWIS MANUEL
432 Juniper Street
Ft. Collins, CO 80521
(303) 223-0012

OBJECTIVE
A Laboratory Technician position

PROFESSIONAL EXPERIENCE

UNIVERSITY OF COLORADO, Boulder, CO   1987-present
Senior Laboratory Technician
- Perform hematological and serological procedures utilizing state-of-the-art automated instrumentation for analytical procedure involved.
- Transplant and maintain embryonic cells and tissue culture.
- Plant, harvest, stain, and take pictures of chromosome cultures using the photomicroscope, and measure chromosome are lengths using the X-Y Digitizer.
- Prepare hyperbaric chambers, equipment and perfusate solutions used in clinical and experimental organ transplantation and preservation.
- Perform routine histology procedures, special staining and handle special tissues.
- Collect field sampling of invertebrates, plants and obtain animals.
- Process laboratory samples for analysis including drying, weighing, dissolving, filtering, separating, mounting, identifying, preserving, and culturing.
- Perform difficult analyses of soils and plants; animal and human body fluids, fats, cells, proteins and tissues; invertebrates; foods.
- Operate complex laboratory instruments and equipment.
- Prepare cultures, reagents, and solutions; specimens and slides.
- Maintain bacterial stock cultures in lyophilized and frozen form.
- Clean and maintain laboratory and work areas; repair laboratory equipment.

COLORADO STATE UNIVERSITY, Ft. Collins, CO   Summers 1985-87
Laboratory Technician
- Provide technical assistance to technicians with student experiments.
- Assist supervisor with laboratory personnel in field sampling.
- Help technician with preparation of various aids for teaching purposes.
- Assist senior lab technician in designing and constructing equipment for various projects.
- Help technicians in the development and execution of research designs.
- Care for animals used in experiments and research.
- Assist with embalming and latex specimens.
- Provide assistance to supervisor in preparing records and other data for computer processing.

EDUCATION
Certified Medical Lab Technician, 1987
T.H. Pickens Tech Center, Aurora, CO

STEPHANIE JANE WILBER
Marriage, Family & Child Counselor
20450 Laguna Niguel Way
Santa Barbara, CA 93103
(805) 963-2393

PROFESSIONAL EXPERIENCE

Marriage, Family & Child Counseling
- Provide crisis intervention, brief and long term counseling to:
  -individual adults -adolescents -couples -families -groups
- Assess, diagnose and treat clients in major life transitions.
- Conduct group therapy series focused on peer counseling, communication and self esteem.
- Educate, assess and counsel women who must decide between abortion, adoption or keeping the child.
- Faciliate all phases of open independent adoptions; supply community referral resources.
- Coordinate intakes, referrals, correspondence, case records.

Chemical Dependency Counseling & Assessment
- Develop and implement primary education on predictable course of recovery for chemical dependency patients focusing on the following:
  Overview of addiction, indicators of potential relapse, self esteem, addiction as a family disease, denial, co-dependency and congruent communication.
- Counsel couples, individuals, families, family groups and adult children of alcoholics during their participation in a 12-Step Program.
- Educate and counsel battered women, demonstrating the relationship between substance abuse and family violence.

EDUCATION
MA Degree - Counseling Psychology - 1984
Pacifica Graduate Institute, Santa Barbara, CA

SPECIAL TRAINING
- California MFCC License #MFC24707 since 1988.
- Assessment and Treatment of Alcoholism.
- Assessment and Treatment of Adult Children of Alcoholics.
- Diagnosis and treatment of child abuse.
- Attended 7-day workshops; Jay Haley, Virginia Satir, Carl Whitaker, Salvador Minuchin and Claudia Black.
- Gained knowledge through personal psychotherapy including:
  Couples Counseling and Gestalt Group Therapy.

EMPLOYMENT HISTORY
Adoption Counselor, Santa Barbara Adoption Center	1989-present
Substance Abuse Consultant, Shelter Services for Women, SB, CA	1986-89
Relaxation Trainer, Cottage Care Center, Santa Barbara, CA	1979-86

KERRY KESSINGER
PO Box 334
Carpinteria, CA 93013
(805) 684-1113

OBJECTIVE   **A Back Office Medical Assistant for a private practice**

**PROFESSIONAL
EXPERIENCE**

1984-92   MEDICAL ASSISTANT
                 <u>Cole & Randall Medical Corporation</u>, Ventura, CA

<u>Back Office Skills</u>
- Assisted in preparing and administering medications, Venipuncture, basic Hematology, Urinalysis and vital signs.
- Assisted doctor with physical examinations.
- Prepared laboratory specimens, electrocardiograms and pulmonary function.
- Sterilized medical equipment.

<u>Front Office Skills</u>
- Typed, transcribed, edited and finalized correspondence on the IBM compatible word processor.
- Prepared insurance billing and collections, bank statements, bookkeeping and cash flow.
- Maintained inventory and filed patient records.
- Supervised and trained temporary staff members, answered phones and greeted patients.

OFFICE SKILLS   IBM PC Computer, word processing, accounting and medical billing, 10-key by touch, calculator, medical terminology, transcription, phone skills, Autoclave, microscope, EKG, cash register, insurance forms, office management and supervision. Typing speed: 65 wpm

EDUCATION   **Medical Assistant Certificate**
                <u>Santa Barbara Business College</u>, 1984

KRISTY LISA MARLIN
1238 Rogers Street
Greeley, CO 80631
(303) 421-0034

OBJECTIVE
A Medical Technologist position

PROFESSIONAL EXPERIENCE
MEDICAL TECHNOLOGIST   1985-present
North Colorado Medical Center, Greeley, CO

- Evaluate trauma situations and prioritize lab work and decide if another technologist is needed to help with the workload to meet strict deadline schedules.

- Complete STAT and urgent lab work with 1-1/2 hour turnaround time for all departments of the lab.

- Finish all lab work coming in within the four hour turnaround time; some work involves running controls and calibrations; log in specimens brought to the lab.

- Perform nightly maintenance required on Paramax, ACA V, ABL-3, ABL-2, Co-oximeter, Gilford Spectrophotometer, Coulter S-Plus.

- Make up controls for chemistry and coagulation.

- Print all instrument runs before 0300 so I have a hard copy of work done before all computers go down; call panic valves to nurses or doctors on all test results when computers are down.

- Enter data in computer of work completed.

- Fill water beakers for urinalysis, coagulation and chemistry; put away previous day specimens for Hematology and chemistry; discard old ones.

- Draw blood on patients being admitted to the hospital or on an out-patient basis needing lab work done; may involve verifying auto unit.

- Troubleshoot instruments as problems arise.

EDUCATION
BS Degree, Medical Technology, 1985
University of Colorado, Boulder, CO

Registered Medical Technologist
American Society of Clinical Pathologists (ASCP)

ASHLEY D. DORRET
1100 Rose Lane
Denver, CO 80210
(303) 778-0012

OBJECTIVE
A Medical Technologist position

CURRENT PROFESSIONAL EXPERIENCE

PORTER MEMORIAL HOSPITAL, Denver, CO   1989-present
Medical Technologist
- Analyze patient's body fluids for chemical constituents, drug levels, hormone levels and cellular elements accurately and in a timely manner.

- Prepare body fluid for analysis; standardize instruments, perform quality control, process patient's sample and report the value(s) obtained.

- Troubleshoot and repair instruments.

- Calibrate procedures and reagent kits.

- Research new procedures.

- Review quality control and solve problems concerning shifts.

- Report panic values according to lab policy.

- Draw blood samples from patients.

- Enter accurate data of completed work into computer system.

EDUCATION
BS Degree, Medical Technology, 1989
University of Colorado, Boulder, CO

Registered Medical Technologist
American Society of Clinical Pathologists (ASCP)

PREVIOUS EMPLOYMENT HISTORY
Home Management, Study, Research, Pueblo, CO   1985-89
Lab Assistant, Denver General Hospital, Denver, CO   1980-85

OLIVIA S. BERGLANDER
2390 Laguna Road
Denver, CO 80210
(303) 778-2234

OBJECTIVE
A Medical Technologist position

CURRENT PROFESSIONAL EXPERIENCE

MEDICAL TECHNOLOGIST, Denver, CO   1984-present
University Hospital, Denver, CO

- Perform and evaluate laboratory procedures accurately within a specific time using quality control as a basis for sending out laboratory analyses.

- Troubleshoot any and all of the chemistry analyzers plus hand-method including analyzing problems, instituting solutions, monitoring and repairing.

- Organize daily workload effectively; complete outstanding work and solve problems from previous shifts.

- Set up and prepare groundwork for new procedures including analyzing, evaluating and concluding from new data.

- Maintain inventory of supplies for each section of the chemistry department; make up daily reagents.

- Perform preventive maintenance on all machines on a daily, weekly, monthly and yearly basis.

- Communicate extremely abnormal test results or any existing concern with a given specimen such as blood contamination to doctor or charge nurse.

- Set up new equipment; conduct training sessions with other technicians.

- Monitor quality control; evaluate and locate problems; find solutions.

- Train new personnel and medical technologist students.

EDUCATION
BS Degree, Medical Technologist, 1984
University of Colorado, Boulder, CO

Registered Medical Technologist
American Society of Clinical Pathologists (ASCP)

SHEILA ANN WHITE
321 West Meadow Drive
Vail, CO 81657
(303) 479-2221

OBJECTIVE
A Medical Technologist position for a medical center

PROFESSIONAL EXPERIENCE

MEDICAL TECHNOLOGIST II
1986-present
Vail Valley Medical Center, Vail, CO

- Establish priorities and schedule, assign and review work of lab personnel.
- Provide technical assistance in resolving problems relating to methods, techniques, instrumentation, and use of equipment.
- Participate in selecting, orienting, training, and evaluating work of lab personnel.
- Perform a variety of tests, evaluate/implement new and modified procedures/tests.
- Developed and maintained an effective quality control program.
- Established/supervised a preventive maintenance program for laboratory equipment.
- Evaluate effectiveness of new equipment and instruments.
- Maintain inventory, prepare cost estimates, establish supply level and order supplies and equipment.
- Review and prepare reports of laboratory activities.
- Assist staff in performing tests; research and instruct in laboratory procedures.

PROFESSIONAL PROFILE

- Gained thorough knowledge of standard laboratory instruments, equipment and techniques.
- Skilled in preparing instructional, research and test specimens using and demonstrating proper procedures and interpreting results.
- Ability to supervise and participate in laboratory work effectively.
- Special talent for resolving difficult problems.
- Ability to establish and maintain effective staff relations; to express myself, clearly and concisely; both orally and in writing.

EDUCATION

BS Degree, Medical Technology, 1985
University of Colorado
Boulder, CO

Registered Medical Technologist
American Society of Clinical Pathologists (ASCP)

ELANA SUZANNE MURPHY
213 Main Street
Spearfish, SD 57783
(605) 642-1111

OBJECTIVE
A Medical Technologist position

PROFESSIONAL EXPERIENCE

MEDICAL TECHNOLOGIST II   1987-present
Lookout Memorial Hospital, Spearfish, SD
- Perform specialized complex and standard laboratory tests.
- Assist staff with research projects; perform and direct necessary tests.
- Prepare and select slides and gross organ displays for instructional materials.
- Ensure quality control throughout the laboratory.
- Monitor test results for consistency and correct actions as needed.
- Orient and train new employees on laboratory operations including automated equipment and on-line computers.
- Perform maintenance, calibration and repair of sophisticated laboratory equipment.
- Order laboratory supplies and equipment.
- Establish reorders, vendor contacts and determine trial of new items.
- Participate on special projects of research and development.

MEDICAL TECHNOLOGIST I   1985-87
Memorial Hospital of Sweetwater County, Rock Springs, WY
- Perform a variety of standard laboratory tests.
- Collect and prepare specimens; set up, standardize and ensure quality control of instruments, equipment and test methods.
- Record data, compute and report test results.
- Analyze blood, urine and other body fluids for chemical constituents through automated instruments and manual techniques including:
  - colorimeters, spectrophotometers, densitometers, fluorometers, osmometers and scintillation counters.
- Count cells from blood and other body fluids; identify, using a microscope, cells and other formed constituents of blood, urine and body fluids.
- Evaluate cellular morphology and inter-relationship of cell types.
- Perform coagulation tests and other tests related to physiologic function by chemical, serologic or immunologic methods.

EDUCATION
BS Degree, Medical Technology, 1984
University of Colorado, Boulder, CO

Registered Medical Technologist
American Society of Clinical Pathologists (ASCP)

RANDY JOSEPH STEPHENSON
3245 9th Street
Denver, CO 80262
(303) 270-1123

OBJECTIVE
A Senior Medical Technologist position

PROFESSIONAL EXPERIENCE

UNIVERSITY HOSPITAL, Denver, CO   1987-present
Senior Medical Technologist
- Perform complex and non-routine tests requiring advanced analytical skills and specialized equipment.
- Facilitate supervision and administrate personnel in assigned laboratory area.
- Serve as main resource person to assist medical technologist staff in resolving problems and establishing protocols, assuring adequate quality control standards.
- Distinguish abnormal test results and other unusual conditions associated with the patient population.
- Recognize unusual problems related to technical methods, instruments, specimens and identify their causes.
- Verify unusual test results through correlation with other laboratory data, patient data, and clarification from clinicians.
- Consult with physicians concerning test protocols and results on a regular basis.
- Collect, analyze, interpret, and display data related to new improved test methods, instruments, and procedures; design research projects.
- Develop user interactive computer programs in the laboratory.
- Prepare and edit documents and manuals to assure proper performance of tests.
- Conduct special training for laboratory staff; participate in didactic sessions and presentation in a Medical Technology Academic Program.
- Perform non-routine maintenance, calibration, and repair of laboratory equipment.
- Design and implement overall systems for quality control, proficiency testing, quality assurance and regulatory standards.

EDUCATION
BS Degree, Medical Technology, 1984
University of Colorado, Boulder, CO

Registered Medical Technologist
American Society of Clinical Pathologists (ASCP)

PREVIOUS WORK EXPERIENCE
Medical Technologist II, Children's Hospital, Denver, CO   1986-87
Medical Technologist I, Humana Hospital, Aurora, CO   1984-86
Medical Technology Intern, UC Medical Center   1982-84

ALLIE S. PATTON
2980 Kittery Court
Ft. Collins, CO 80526
(303) 223-0039

OBJECTIVE
A Medical Transcriptionist position

CURRENT PROFESSIONAL EXPERIENCE

MEDICAL TRANSCRIPTIONIST   1986-present
Lutheran Medical Center, Wheat Ridge, CO
* Type all daily transcription for surgical out-patients and papsmears.

* Type, update and file cards accurately for each case.

* Pull and send slides for physician consultation.

* Ensure that the Mammogram Center has copies of all breast cases.

* Answer phones and transfer calls to appropriate person.

* Give diagnosis over the phone to hospital doctors, private practitioners and patients.

* Separate reports for charting and billing.

* Chart pathological reports in proper patient chart.

* Copy records for billing and cancer file; update cancer file monthly.

* Type autopsies, requesting proper charts and papers for the procedure.

* Pick up and distribute laboratory mail.

EDUCATION
Certified Medical Transcriptionist, 1986
Boulder Valley Voc-Tech Center
Boulder, CO

PREVIOUS EMPLOYMENT HISTORY
Personnel Assistant, University Hospital, Denver, CO   1984-86
Word Processor, Denver General Hospital, Denver, CO   1982-84
Medical Secretary, Poudre Valley Hospital, Ft. Collins, CO   1978-82

KATHY ANNE SANDS
1938 Canyon Avenue
Lakewood, CO 80215
(303) 232-8876

OBJECTIVE
A Medical Transcriptionist position

CURRENT PROFESSIONAL EXPERIENCE

HOSPICE OF SAINT JOHN, Lakewood, CO   1988-present
Senior Medical Transcriptionist

- Transcribe patient's medical records as dictated by staff physicians. Transcription involves listening, typing, memorizing, storing, proofreading and printing material.

- Provide daily supervision of transcription section of Medical Records Department.

- Complete editing functions for computerized dictating system.

- Communicate regularly with department head on status of transcription section.

- Distribute typed reports and utilize hospital computer to obtain needed information.

- Maintain records of production for the transcription section.

- Schedule work and vacation/holiday hours for transcription section.

- Provide educational opportunities for transcriptionists through inservices.

- Evaluate equipment problems, call for service, and maintain records of repairs.

- Obtain charts for physicians, answer phones; complete requests in clerk's absence.

- Test job applicants and train employees on word processing and dictating system.

EDUCATION
Medical Office Transcription
Medical Careers Training Center
Ft. Collins, CO Certified 1986

PREVIOUS EMPLOYMENT HISTORY
Medical Transcriptionist, University Hospital, Denver, CO   1986-88
Administrative Assistant, Poudre Valley Hospital, Ft. Collins, CO   1983-86
Word Processor, Goleta Valley Hospital, Goleta, CA   1980-83

SARA O'REILLY
321 Denning Court
Denver, CO 80204
(303) 629-3321

OBJECTIVE
A Mental Health Technician position

CURRENT PROFESSIONAL EXPERIENCE

DENVER GENERAL HOSPITAL, Denver, CO   1988-present
Mental Health Technician
- Assist patients in activities of daily living including personal hygiene, making beds, dressing, eating and play.

- Work as a team to meet the physical, emotional, environmental and social needs of psychiatric patients.

- Observe, report and document patient behavior and interactions with others.

- Give patients medications.

- Help patients receiving ECT prepare for treatment and recovery.

- Assist nurse with implementation and documentation of seclusion procedures and suicide precautions.

- Help staff with medical emergencies under strict supervision.

- Take and record patients' vital signs; collect specimens to deliver to lab.

- Assist in managing assaultive or confused patients; implement restraining procedures when necessary.

EDUCATION
Mental Health Technician, 1982
Pueblo Community College
Pueblo, CO

PREVIOUS EMPLOYMENT HISTORY
Psychiatric Aide, Mental Health Center, Boulder, CO   1986-88
Mental Health Aide, Jefferson Ctr for Mental Health, Arvada, CO 1983-86
Nursing Aide, Denver Nursing Home, Littleton, CO   1982-83

JOYCE ALAINE HUMPHREY
9087 Robin Drive
Denver, CO 80222
(303) 692-1110

OBJECTIVE
A Music Therapist position

CURRENT PROFESSIONAL EXPERIENCE

SPAULDING REHABILITATION HOSPITAL   1986-present
Music Therapist

- Assess lifeskills and pediatrics rehabilitation patients for appropriateness to receive music therapy treatment.

- Plan and articulate written treatment plans for patients.

- Execute group and individual music therapy treatment sessions.

- Document treatment and progress of patients.

- Attend and participate in staffings, rounds and family conferences.

- Provide inservices to staff and departments regarding music therapy.

- Create tapes and other music related equipment to enhance programming.

EDUCATION

BS Degree, Music Therapy, 1980
Colorado State University, Ft. Collins, CO

AAS Degree, Nursing, 1976
Front Range Community College
Westminister Campus, CO

PREVIOUS EMPLOYMENT HISTORY

Music Therapist, Humana Hospital, Aurora, CO   1983-86
Music Therapist, Denver General Hospital, Denver, CO   1980-83
Staff Nurse, Poudre Valley Hospital, Ft. Collins, CO   1976-80

DANIEL STAN WEISS
222 East Folsum Street
Denver, CO 80210
(303) 778-2222

OBJECTIVE
A Nuclear Medicine Technologist position

PROFESSIONAL EXPERIENCE

PORTER MEMORIAL HOSPITAL, Denver, CO   1984-present
<u>Nuclear Medical Technologist</u>

- Trace radioactive substance that is usually injected; use gamma cameras and highly sophisticated computerized equipment.

- Practice radiation safety; document all radioactivity received, used and disposed.

- Schedule patients for a variety of scans and coordinate X-ray for examinations.

- Prepare and administer radiopharmaceuticals to patients.

- Maintain all records of delivery; use and dispose radioactive materials as approved by the State of Colorado Health Department.

- Educate radiology patients concerning the how's, why's and time involved.

- Position patients correctly to make them as comfortable as possible.

- Meet with radiopharmaceutical sales people to keep up-to-date with medicines and to purchase the best products at the lowest possible prices.

- Order all supplies and keep room neat, clean, and contamination free.

- Compose policy and procedures for nuclear medicine in accordance with hospital and Colorado State Health.

- Keep up-to-date on nuclear medicine education, CPR, tapes, videos and seminars.

EDUCATION
AAS Degree, Nuclear Medical Technology, 1980
<u>Community College of Denver</u>, Denver, CO

PREVIOUS EMPLOYMENT HISTORY
Radiologic Technologist, <u>General Hospital</u>, Denver, CO   1982-84
Ultrasound Technologist, <u>UC Medical Center</u>, Denver, CO   1981-82
Clinical Lab Technologist, <u>University Hospital</u>, Denver, CO   1979-81

JODY LUANNE VICTOR
2009 Park Place
Aurora, CO 80012
(303) 695-0211

OBJECTIVE
A Staff Nurse position

CURRENT PROFESSIONAL EXPERIENCE

HUMANA HOSPITAL, Aurora, CO   1990-present
Registered Nurse I

- Provide direct patient care; keep legal documents of nurses notes and maintain adequate communication among patient care staff.

- Administer medications to patients, i.e., IV, PO, rectal and topical.

- Complete prescribed treatments including dosage changes, accuchecks, and ambulation.

- Serve as liaison between patient and doctor.

- Provide teaching to patient and family on procedures and disease process.

- Maintain a positive image for the hospital to families, patient and community.

- Develop and follow through on patient care plans.

- Provide emotional support for families and patients when they most need it.

- Recognize patient needs for discharge including home nursing and meals-on-wheels.

- Make judgments on patient conditions and call doctors based on those decisions.

EDUCATION
AAS Degree, Nursing, 1988
Front Range Community College
Ft. Collins, CO

PREVIOUS EMPLOYMENT HISTORY
Staff Nurse, UC Medical Center, Denver, CO   1989-90
Clinical Nurse, Boulder Youth Clinic, Boulder, CO   1988-89

SHIELA L. LORIE
1940 Parkwood Place
Ft. Collins, CO 80524
(303) 224-0594

OBJECTIVE
A Staff Nurse position at a hospital

CURRENT PROFESSIONAL EXPERIENCE

UNIVERSITY HOSPITAL, Denver, CO   1989-present
Registered Nurse I
- Administer medications and monitor results on a routine and as needed basis to 4-7 patients per night in the Surgical Unit.

- Check vital signs each night.

- Assess each assigned patient for skin integrity, lung sounds, bowel sounds, wounds, and IV site.

- Administer IV fluids and medications including antibiotics, TPN, narcotics; monitor results looking for potential side effects, adverse reactions and pain.

- Monitor lab data, blood work, urinalysis and report and critical data.

- Report to next shift, care given and patient's condition; document all care given in patient's chart.

- Perform sterile procedures including catheterization and dressing changes.

- Assess patients on admission.

- Administer blood and blood products; document any side effects.

EDUCATION
AAS Degree, Nursing, 1986
Front Range Community College
Westminster, CO

PREVIOUS EMPLOYMENT HISTORY
Staff Nurse, Denver General Hospital, Denver, CO   1988-89
Staff Nurse, Memorial Hospital, Colorado Springs, CO   1986-88

NANCY I. NUNNALLY
3860 Kittery Court
Ft. Collins, CO 80525
(303) 224-9954

OBJECTIVE
A Registered Nurse position in the Special Care Nursery

CURRENT PROFESSIONAL EXPERIENCE

POUDRE VALLEY HOSPITAL, Ft. Collins, CO   1985-present
Registered Nurse II
* Provide skilled nursing care for critical and non-critically ill newborns.

* Attend deliveries to care for the baby and assess all newborns.

* Start IV's on infants.

* Draw blood from infants for basic lab work and arterial blood gases.

* Gavage feedings for premature infants.

* Develop a patient care plan for each newborn.

* Care for normal healthy newborns; teach baby care to new parents.

* Orient students and new employees.

* Assist the physician with procedures and keep the work area sterilized.

EDUCATION
BS Degree, Nursing, 1981
University of Northern Colorado
Greeley, CO

Critical Care Nursing Certificate
West Valley College
Saratoga, CA

PREVIOUS EMPLOYMENT HISTORY
Staff Nurse, UC Medical Center, Denver, CO   1984-85
Staff Nurse, Denver General Hospital, Denver, CO   1981-84

MADELINE R. SWIFT
3967 Telephone Road
Denver, CO 80204
(303) 629-8754

OBJECTIVE
A Registered Nursing position in a hospital Nursery Unit

CURRENT PROFESSIONAL EXPERIENCE
DENVER GENERAL HOSPITAL, Denver, CO   1988-present
Registered Nurse II

- Attend deliveries in the birth unit; assess condition and resuscitate newborns immediately after birth.

- Assess and care for premature newborn and sick babies; collaborate with physicians concerning care of infants.

- Initiate babies' feedings; breast and nipple feedings; assist parents with problems.

- Assess vital signs, feedings and baths; update care plans and initiate conferences and discharge planning.

- Start IV's, draw ABG's and other labor work; collect specimens, assist with procedures.

- Monitor equipment including AVI pumps, cardiac/respiratory monitors, isolletes, open warmers, ventilators, TCM, pulse ox, and oxygen flow meter.

- Educate patients with special care procedures including home monitors, newborn care, and medications.

- Prepare and administer medications.

- Stabilize critical babies and prepare for transport to Denver.

EDUCATION
BS Degree, Nursing, 1979
University of Colorado, Boulder, CO

Critical Care Nursing Certificate
West Valley College, Saratoga, CA

PREVIOUS EMPLOYMENT HISTORY
Staff Nurse, Saint Joseph Hospital, Denver, CO   1984-88
Staff Nurse, North Colorado Medical Center, Greeley, CO   1979-84

JORDANA C. WADE
2109 Whitsett Street
Denver, CO 80210
(303) 778-0009

OBJECTIVE
A Registered Nurse position

CURRENT PROFESSIONAL EXPERIENCE

POUDRE VALLEY HOSPITAL, Ft. Collins, CO   1985-present
Registered Nurse II
- Perform routine exams and charting of newborns using APGAR rating, EGA tool and physician exam.
- Provide IV therapy; Start IV, monitor site, rate, additives, change tubing and solution.
- Give medications by mouth, IM or IV including calculating amounts from dosages.
- Evaluate nipple feedings; prepare warm formulas; assist with breastfeeding; place and give oral and gastric tube feedings per schedule; monitor blood sugar.
- Set up ventilator therapy.
- Give and receive shift report to oncoming staff with emphasis on evaluation of care and writing further plans for care.
- Attend deliveries including C-sections and natural childbirth; assure resuscitation equipment is set up; assess newborn and determine need for more intensive care.
- Consult with parents, lab, doctors and other disciplines to arrange for procedures, give updates, and advice to parents.
- Obtain specimens; blood by heel/toe sticks, central venous draws, umbilical artery catheter, arterial veins; place urine bag for spec. and output measurements.
- Perform routine physical assessment; take temperature, pulse, respirations, and blood pressure on a set schedule and notify doctor.
- Serve as liaison for parents between doctors and other disciplines.
- Restock equipment to patient areas and supply carts; collect laundry; prepare patient charges.

EDUCATION
BS Degree, Nursing, 1979
University of Northern Colorado
Greeley, CO

Critical Care Nursing Certificate
West Valley College, Saratoga, CA

PREVIOUS EMPLOYMENT HISTORY
Staff Nurse, Denver General Hospital, Denver, CO   1981-85
Staff Nurse, Porter Memorial Hospital, Denver, CO   1979-81

CYNTHIA C. CROWLEY
3994 Baseline Road
Boulder, CO, 80302
(303) 440-0023

OBJECTIVE
A Clinical Nursing position

CURRENT PROFESSIONAL EXPERIENCE

BOULDER COMMUNITY HOSPITAL, Boulder, CO   1986-present
Registered Nurse II, Surgical Unit

- Provide high quality, skilled and professional nursing care.

- Identify a wide range of complex patient care problems and implement nursing interventions, evaluating the results.

- Teach patient pre- and post operation procedures.

- Coordinate discharge procedures.

- Dispense patient medications carefully without error.

- Inform the physician of patient's status by phone, in person and by charting.

- Prepare reports to relay patient care information to the next shift.

- Plan individualized patient care and type into computer.

- Document all care given in patient's chart.

- Serve as patient advocate and provide emotional support.

- Orient new employees.

EDUCATION
AAS Degree, Nursing 1984
Front Range Community College
Westminster, CO

PREVIOUS EMPLOYMENT HISTORY

Clinical Nurse, Porter Memorial Hospital, Denver, CO   1985-86
Clinical Nurse, North Colorado Medical Center, Greeley, CO   1984-85

ANGELA DeROSSI
4966 Peterson Street
Ft. Collins, CO 80524
(303) 224-9954

OBJECTIVE
A Clinical Nurse position

CURRENT PROFESSIONAL EXPERIENCE
REGISTERED NURSE III   1982-present
University Hospital, Denver, CO

- Serve as charge nurse, performing orthopedic nursing skills without supervision.
- Identify complex patient care problems noting subtle changes in clinical status and anticipating outcome of nursing interventions.
- Develop and record nursing care plans for all patients; conduct patient care conferences while serving as resource person.
- Serve as preceptor for RN, AD/Diploma/BSN and refresher student nursing program.
- Utilize approaches and techniques to accomplish stated goals and objectives while coordinating patient care with other health care professionals.
- Evaluate and document effectiveness of patient care plan and degree of goal attainment; revise as necessary.
- Provide counseling, guidance and appropriate referrals for patients, families and all care givers.
- Give input to revise existing department policies and procedures.
- Plan and participate on agenda for floor meetings.
- Teach patient/family development, a written program in the nursing care plan; assure continuity.
- Function as chairperson of nursing and hospital committees including the audit committee for the orthopedic unit.
- Teach CPR in the Education Department and keep orthopedic unit up-to-date with CPR procedures.

PROFESSIONAL PROFILE
- Ability to perform unit specific system-by-system patient assessment.
- Enhance hospital image by exhibiting diplomacy with others.
- Completed 80 hours of annual related inservice. (20 hours is required.)

EDUCATION
AAS Degree Nursing, 1977
Front Range Community College, Westminster, CO

PREVIOUS EMPLOYMENT HISTORY
Staff Nurse, Poudre Valley Hospital, Ft. Collins, CO   1979-82
Staff Nurse, Denver General Hospital, Denver, CO   1877-78

RHONDA N. SEGAL
1110 California Street
Denver, CO 80210
(303) 778-0002

OBJECTIVE
A Staff Clinical Nurse position

CURRENT PROFESSIONAL EXPERIENCE

CLINICAL REGISTERED NURSE III   1983-present
Porter Memorial Hospital, Denver, CO
- Assess patient condition based on objective signs, symptoms, and subjective data as verbalized by patient.
- Plan patient care based on his/her level of wellness and potential for recovery.
- Implement plan of care and assure consistency throughout shifts to carry out.
- Evaluate how the plan of care is progressing and if changes need to be made.
- Interact with family, physicians and other disciplines regarding the patient and plan of care.
- Carry out procedures as ordered by physician in order to help patient achieve a higher level of wellness or maintain patient's present level of wellness.
- Prep patient for X-ray or surgery, medications, and IV's.
- Teach patients about their health and how to prevent future problems as well as ways to enhance or maintain their present level of wellness.
- Serve as a change agent for the patient if things in his/her plan of care need to be altered to promote a higher level of wellness.
- Act as patient's advocate while in the hospital, making sure that he/she is receiving the best possible care.
- Serve as role model for fellow workers, new employees and student interns.
- Participate in committees and staff meetings to enhance nursing and patient care; collaborate with other shifts and disciplines to promote better patient care.

EDUCATION
BS Degree, Nursing, 1978
University of Northern Colorado, Greeley, CO

Certified Nursing Assistant, 1974
Aims College, Greeley, CO

PREVIOUS EMPLOYMENT HISTORY
Staff Nurse, Swedish Medical Center, Denver, CO   1980-83
Staff Nurse, UC Medical Center, Denver, CO   1978-79
Nursing Assistant, Boulder Community Hospital, Boulder, CO   1974-78

ANNA S. FARLEY
335 Rocky Creek Road
Boise, ID, 83712
(208) 342-9990

Lieutenant Colonel
Idaho Air National Guard
125th USAF Clinic, Riverton, ID

OBJECTIVE: A Clinical Civilian Nurse in a <u>U.S. Military Health Care Facility</u>.

**LICENSE/
EDUCATION:**

BS Degree - Nursing, 1973 - Summa Cum Laude
<u>Idaho State University</u>, Boise, ID

Registered Nurse, <u>State of Idaho</u> (A123456)
State of Idaho Standard Lifetime Services Credential

**MILITARY
TRAINING:**

- Nursing Service Management for Air Reserve Forces, 1985
- Air Command and Staff College, 1982
- Regular attendance, Association of Military Surgeons of the United States.
- Regular attendance, annual active duty, USAF hospitals in the Western United States.

EXPERIENCE:

1986-present   **CLINICAL NURSE (RN)**, <u>County of Boise</u>, Health Care Services, Boise, ID.   Provide health care services to 18,000 patients (annually) in numerous clinics throughout the facility: Family Planning, Tuberculosis screening and referral, Well Baby Clinics (CHDP), Immunizations, Pregnancy Testing, counseling and referral, Primary Care, <u>total</u> Obstetrical Outpatient care, Blood Pressure screening.   Operate clinical laboratory, ordering and maintaining supplies, compiling statistics, supervision of service aides, triage, crisis intervention including psychiatric, social/medical referral, pre/post HIV counseling.

1974-76   **MIGRANT NURSE (PHN)**, <u>Boise County Department of Education Migrant Education Program</u>, Boise, ID.   Traveled extensively throughout the valley area to provide health care services, physical exams, referral and follow-up care to children qualifying under Migrant Services and AFDC funding.   Developed working knowledge of Spanish.

AFFILIATIONS:

- Association of Medical Surgeons of the United States
- Air National Guard Association
- ANG Nurses Association

LISA HEATHER HUNTER
4590 Mountain Creek Road
Oceanside, CA 90266
(619) 630-4582

OBJECTIVE
A Nursing position in an OB/GYN clinic environment

PROFESSIONAL EXPERIENCE

FETAL MONITORING SERVICES, San Diego, CA   1990-present
Antepartum Consultant
- Perform 25-50 non-stress tests per month for the County of San Diego and provide testing for several private physicians.

GENERAL HOSPITAL, San Diego, CA   1977-present
Obstetrical & Out-Patient Nurse
- Provide total patient care and support and during the antepartum, labor and delivery process for eight years.
  - Counsel and educate patients in labor, postpartum and newborn care.
  - Assessed and triaged incoming labor patients.
  - Assisted doctor with delivery and provide immediate newborn care.
  - Managed obstetrical emergency intervention.
- Provide total to postpartum and long-term antepartum patients on the mother-infant unit.
- Provide complete care for short-term surgery patients...
  Admitting...circulating...recovering...discharge planning.

Administration & Management
- Charge nurse for the labor and delivery unit; 120-160 births per month.
  - Supervised and scheduled a staff of 18 nurses.
  - Interviewed, hired and oriented new personnel.
- Oversaw the Antepartum testing unit.
  - Assisted in developing effective antepartum policies and procedures.
  - Performed NSTs, OCTs, BSTs and assisted with fetal versions and amnio-centesis.

EDUCATION
BS Degree, Nursing, 1974
Humboldt State University

LICENSE/CERTIFICATE
- California State Nursing License #678910
- Public Health Certificate, #1234

NANCY DWORKIN, R.N.
5567 Santa Monica Blvd
Los Angeles, CA 90067
(213) 344-9999

Objective: Occupational Health Nurse

PROFESSIONAL EXPERIENCE

Occupational Health Nurse
- Established and maintained health care programs for two manufacturing corporations each employing over 1500 employees for a one-nurse office.
  - Provided and performed emergency first aid, pre-employment physical examinations and Worker's Compensation cases on a daily basis.
  - Prepared and maintained all medical records and OSHA reports.
- Conducted in-house CPR and first aid classes for all employees.
- Developed safety programs and participated in Safety Committee meetings.
- Provided continued medical treatment, working closely with clinics and hospitals throughout the community.
- Performed services for the Rehabilitation Program and routine follow-up.
- Interacted with all levels of management personnel in a professional and diplomatic manner.
- Purchased and maintained inventory/quality control of all clinical equipment and supplies.

Acute Emergency Assessment & Intervention
- Superior performance in critical care unit; general..medical..surgical..coronary care..post trauma..neurological..gerontological..open heart surgeries.
- Expert in management of pain control and hyperalimentation (TPN).
- Assessed patient's physiological, emotional and social needs.
  - Ability to quickly determine and perform the best care possible.
- Thoroughly skilled in family dynamics to effectively counsel patients and offer emotional/spiritual support to the terminally ill and their families.

EDUCATION
BS Degree, Psychology/Registered Nurse
University of Minas Gerais, Brazil
Critical Care Nursing Certificate
West Valley College, Saratoga, CA
MBO Certificate, Business Administration
University of California, San Diego
Intensive Care/Rehabilitation
Santa Clara Valley Medical Center, SC, CA

EMPLOYMENT HISTORY

Occupational Health Nurse, Medical Research Inc, Carson, CA	1989-91
Intensive Care Nurse, VA Hospital, Los Angeles, CA	1978-89
Staff Nurse, Carroll's SNF Lexington, San Diego, CA	1977-78

MARIANNE S. KENT
2038 Magnolia Street
Ft. Collins, CO 80524
(303) 224-6667

Objective: A Pediatric ICU Nurse Management position

PROFESSIONAL PROFILE
- 10+ years experience in the pediatric nursing profession.
- Member, American Nurses Association since 1979.
- Member, Society of Head & Neck Nurses, 1982-84.

PROFESSIONAL EXPERIENCE

Management & Supervision
- In charge of an outpatient pediatric Otolaryngology (OTO) Clinic.
- Increased patient load by 50 percent.
- Instituted an outpatient ear tube placement clinic.
- Strengthened the role of the professional nurse by increasing patient teaching and telephone support.
- Interviewed, hired, trained, supervised nursing and clerical staff.
- Supported and facilitated residence-in-training.

Patient Education & Counseling
- Developed and implemented a patient educational program for mothers and children on Interferon Drug Study.
- Wrote a baby care booklet for participants in an alcohol & pregnancy project.
- Counseled mothers in child development on a one-on-one basis.
- Developed and utilized a patient training education film for outpatient surgery of a Pediatric Otolaryngology Clinic.
- Revised surgery pamphlets on OTO procedures.
- Conducted biweekly outpatient pre-op hospital tours.

Acute Nursing Care
- Provided care to critically ill children in a medical/surgical setting.
- Served as staff nurse on an adolescent surgery unit and worked with complicated post-op surgical procedures.

EDUCATION/LICENSE
Colorado State Nursing License
BSN, Denver Children's Hospital, 1980
BA, Psychology, Denver College, Denver, CO, 1978

EMPLOYMENT HISTORY

Pediatric Nurse/Staff Manager, Poudre Valley Hospital, Ft. Collins, CO	1990-present
Home Health Care Consultant, Ft. Collins, CO	1985-90
Pediatric Staff Nurse, Children's Hospital, Denver, CO	1980-85
Staff Nurse, Children's Medical Center, Los Angeles, CA	1979-80

THERESA E. CHILDS, RN
6912 Waterloo Lane
Montecito, CA 93108
(805) 569-9992

Objective: A Utilization Review Nurse position.

PROFESSIONAL EXPERIENCE

Administration & Management
- Manage the Comprehensive Perinatal Services Program for Carpinteria and Franklin clinics.
- Supervise the assessment of designated patients for prenatal care:
  - physical...nutrition...psycho-social...and health education.
- Monitor patient care and review documentation to determine accuracy and compliance with California State guidelines.
- Coordinate care for 350 Hispanic and low income Prenatal and Postpartum patients.
- In charge of ordering and interpreting lab tests, triaging and appropriate follow-up within Santa Barbara County protocols.

Acute/Residential Nursing Care
- Performed plasmaphoresis for oncology patients at a 500-bed government hospital.
- Participated in the Oncology Department rounds to ensure appropriate care.
- Charge nurse for a 30-bed unit Chemical Dependency and Acute Medical/ Surgical patients. Monitored care of short-stay surgical patients.
  - Liaison between patient, family and therapy staff and physicians.
  - Worked with PSRO, Medicare and SSI to provide documentation within their guidelines.
- Provided care to developmentally disabled patients in a 200-bed resident facility.
  - Developed individual health care program for residents.
  - Reviewed medical history for resident's admission.

Counselor/Educator
- Counseled and educated HIV testing individuals.
- Provided post pregnancy test counseling to women.
- Educated patients in Diabetes, PIH, AFP screening, PTL, RH sensitization.

EDUCATION
AA Degree, Nursing, Santa Barbara City College, 1975

LICENSE/ORGANIZATIONS
California State Nursing License #A0000
Member, US-Mexico Border Health Association/WHO

EMPLOYMENT HISTORY
OB Clinic Manager, County of Santa Barbara	1983-90
Staff Nurse, Goleta Valley Hospital, Goleta, CA	1978-83
Staff Nurse, Devereaux School, Santa Barbara, CA	1975-76

JOSEPH DARWIN
39850 Balsam Avenue
Boulder, CO 80302
(303) 440-0321

OBJECTIVE
A Nursing Assistant position

CURRENT PROFESSIONAL EXPERIENCE

BOULDER COMMUNITY HOSPITAL, Boulder, CO   1988-present
<u>Certified Nursing Assistant</u>
- Assist nursing staff and X-ray technicians in the Radiology Department.

- Transport patients to and from the Radiology Department safely.

- Take X-ray reports to all nursing wards in the hospital.

- Process X-ray films in the darkroom.

- Move patients from carts or wheelchairs onto X-ray tables.

- Check transport equipment for continued safe operation.

- Maintain cleanliness of hospital wheelchairs and carts.

- Pull X-ray jackets from file rooms and verify exams on the computer.

- Store films and supplies in their proper places.

- Answer phones and take accurate messages.

EDUCATION
Certified Nursing Assistant
<u>Aims College</u>
Greeley, CO Certified: 1980

PREVIOUS EMPLOYMENT HISTORY
Nursing Assistant, <u>Denver General Hospital</u>, Denver, CO   1985-88
Nursing Assistant, <u>Routt Memorial Hospital</u>, Steamboat Springs, CO   1983-85
Nursing Aide, <u>Humana Hospital</u>, Aurora, CO   1980-83

ELEANOR S. WYATT
5920 California Street
Ft. Collins, CO 80522
(303) 223-0947

OBJECTIVE
A Nursing Assistant position

CURRENT PROFESSIONAL EXPERIENCE

NURSING ASSISTANT   1989-present
McKee Medical Center, Loveland, CO
- Assist patients who have had some type of sudden illness or accident resulting in a disability and a change in their life style.

- Help patients achieve their maximum ability, a degree of independence and positive attitude about their life.

- Check patients' vital signs.

- Assist patients with oral hygiene, bathing, dressing and general housekeeping.

- Help patients with proper positioning, transfers and ambulation.

- Transport patients to and from dining room.

- Report any change in patients' condition to the registered nurse in charge.

- Organize and participate in activities with patients on and off the rehabilitation unit such as cooking and playing games.

- Converse with patients and take an interest in their life.

EDUCATION
Certified Nursing Assistant, 1984
Aims College, Greeley, CO

PREVIOUS EMPLOYMENT HISTORY
Nursing Assistant, Mediplex Rehab-Denver, Thornton, CO   1987-89
Nursing Assistant, Estes Park Medical Center, Estes Park, CO   1985-87
Nursing Assistant, Centennial Peaks Hospital, Greeley, CO   1984-85

DIANA E. COLLINS
5510 Statlyn Court
Santa Barbara, CA 93103
(805) 569-1000

Objective: A Director of Nursing position

PROFESSIONAL PROFILE

- 17 years' experience in the health care industry.
- Deal with sensitive situations in a professional and concerned manner.
- Highly organized, dedicated with a positive mental attitude.
- Outstanding written, oral and bilingual communication skills.
- Co-authored an article with Joan Probert, RN, published in the *Journal of Christian Nursing*, Winter 1985.
- Member, Nat'l Hospice Nurses Assn and Nurses Christian Fellowship.
- Gained valuable business and personal contacts throughout the Santa Barbara health care community.

PROFESSIONAL EXPERIENCE

Management & Supervision
- Supervised entire hospital evening nursing staff and became main source for troubleshooting among nursing professionals at St. Francis Hospital.
  - Responsible for overall nursing staff performance and total care of 100 bed facility.
  - Assured that family members were very well informed and involved.
- Supervised home health aides and private duty nurses for hospice home care. Successfully filled in as Director of Nurses in Director's absence.
- Charge nurse on a 40 bed surgical floor for six months.
  - Relief charge nurse of 32 bed floor in a 400 bed hospital for two years.
- Received extensive health care management training.

Hospice Home Care
- Expert in pain control and symptom management for five years.
  - Assessed patient's pain with ability to quickly determine best analgesic and method of delivery.
  - Thoroughly skilled in family dynamics to effectively counsel patients and offer emotional/spiritual support to terminally ill adults and their families.
  - Coordinate overall home care program with other community resources and services throughout Santa Barbara County.

- More -

PROFESSIONAL EXPERIENCE (Continued)

Acute Emergency Assessment & Intervention
- Superior performance in intensive care unit for eight years:
  general..medical..surgical..coronary care..post trauma..neurological
  - Eight year member of the Code Blue Team, responding to cardiac arrest situations throughout the hospital.
  - Served as the only evening shift IV Therapist for three months at a 400 bed facility.
  - Assisted in the Emergency Room as needed.

Foreign/Domestic Community Relations
- Volunteered as a Red Cross Nurse for five years.
- Educated parents as a PEP volunteer. (Post-Partum Education for Parents)
  - Served on the steering committee.
  - Developed a Baby Basics Class for expectant parents.
- Provided health care assistance in a remote clinic in Mexico as a World Health Volunteer.
  - Studied at the Jaime Balmes University in Saltillo, Mexico. Resided with a Mexican family.
- Volunteered through the American Heart Association. (Project Re-Entry)
  - Visited Stroke patients in their homes.
  - Coordinated outpatient therapy, arranged for supportive equipment and offered emotional support.

EDUCATION

AA Degree, Nursing, Sacramento City College, 1972
President, Chapter of the Student Nurses Association

EMPLOYMENT HISTORY

Hospice Nurse/Acting Director, Hospice of Santa Barbara Inc	1984-90
Relief Supervisor/Staff Nurse, St. Francis Hospital	1976-84
Evening Clinic Nurse, Outpatient Clinic, Sacramento, CA	1/76-7/76
IV Therapist/Charge & Staff Nurse, Mercy General Hospital	1972-75

MOLLY RACHEL SUMMERS
4321 Pearl Street
Denver, CO 80229
(303) 893-7000

OBJECTIVE
A Staff Pediatric Occupational Therapist

CURRENT PROFESSIONAL EXPERIENCE
CHILDREN'S HOSPITAL, Denver, CO   1989-present
Pediatric Occupational Therapist
- Evaluate infants and children with physical disabilities.

- Develop and implement individual family service plans and educational programs.

- Fabricate adaptive equipment and splints.

- Consult with and educate parents on how to do the therapy exercises at home and the use of special equipment.

- Supervise physical and occupational therapy staff and student interns.

ACTIVITIES AND HONORS
- Member, Center for the Study of Sensory Integrative Dysfunction
- Kansas University Endowment Association Scholarship, 1976-77
- Boulder Community Hospital Auxiliary Scholarship, 1976-78

EDUCATION
Neurodevelopmental Treatment Pediatric Certification
San Francisco, California, Summer 1986

BS Degree, Occupational Therapy, 1984
University of Kansas, Lawrence, KS

PREVIOUS EMPLOYMENT HISTORY
Pediatric OT, STRIDE Learning Center, Cheyenne, WY   1987-88
Pediatric OT, United Cerebral Palsy Center, Bangor, ME   1986-87
Pediatric OT, Las Cruces Public Schools, Las Cruces, NM   1984-86
OT Internship, Carrie Tingley Hospital-Outreach Program
Las Cruces, NM   Summers 1980-84

CHERYL L. CHARLES
3860 Mathews Street
Ft. Collins, CO 80524
(303) 224-0076

OBJECTIVE
A Staff Psychiatric Occupational Therapist position

CURRENT PROFESSIONAL EXPERIENCE

POUDRE VALLEY HOSPITAL, Ft. Collins, CO   1984-present
Psychiatric Occupational Therapist

- Evaluate patients in the psychiatric unit for the following:
  - cognitive, perceptual/visual motor function, ADLS, independent living skills, job readiness, organization, and brain damage.

- Conduct sessions for the psychiatric unit on media, task, verbal discharge planning, ADL and sensory integration.

- Document patient progress with on-going reports.

- Participate in Team Treatment Plan Meetings and record occupational therapy treatment plan in conjunction with group.

- Interact with other staff members reporting incidents/progress in occupational therapy treatment.

- Supervise unit, maintaining a safe environment for treatment of patient.

- Develop and maintain occupational therapy budget for psychiatric unit.

- Select/order supplies that are appropriate for patients in evaluation and treatment.

- Conduct presentations to groups outside hospital regarding function of occupational therapy in a psychiatric setting.

EDUCATION
MA Degree, Psychology, 1977
University of Colorado, Boulder

BS Degree, Occupational Therapy, 1973
Colorado State University, Ft. Collins, CO

PREVIOUS EMPLOYMENT HISTORY

Occupational Therapist, St. Joseph Hospital, Denver, CO	1979-84
Occupational Therapist, Denver General Hospital, Denver, CO	1973-79

NATALIE S. ROSKY
2850 Rogers Street
Ft. Collins, CO 80525
(303) 223-0009

OBJECTIVE
An Occupational Therapist position

CURRENT PROFESSIONAL EXPERIENCE

DENVER GENERAL HOSPITAL, Denver, CO   1989-present
Registered Occupational Therapist

- Evaluate patients to determine deficits and specific needs for therapy.

- Participate in conferences with physician, interdisciplinary team, patient and family.

- Provide direct patient therapy using the appropriate special equipment when needed; educate patient and family in proper use of special equipment.

- Write reports of patient's progress, discharge evaluation, and ongoing evaluation for physician and/or caregivers.

- Develop new procedures for specific treatment areas.

- Schedule and supervise occupational therapy (OT) students, volunteers and aides.

- Provide information to physicians, community agencies and other hospital employees on the role of the occupational therapist (OT).

- Developed and maintain an efficient computerized OT statistics program.

- Order supplies and maintain inventory of OT library.

EDUCATION
BS Degree, Occupational Therapy, 1984
Colorado State University, Ft. Collins, CO

PREVIOUS EMPLOYMENT HISTORY
Occupational Therapist, Poudre Valley Hospital, Ft. Collins, CO   1984-89
Occupational Therapy Intern, Respite Care, Ft. Collins, CO   1982-84

RHONDA JUNE HART
1212 Taft Hill Road
Ft. Collins, CO 80526
(303) 223-0043

OBJECTIVE
An Occupational Therapist position

CURRENT PROFESSIONAL EXPERIENCE

POUDRE VALLEY HOSPITAL, Ft. Collins, CO   1985-present
Registered Occupational Therapist
- Evaluate, assess and treat infants, children, and adult patients on the Life Skills Rehab Unit (LSR).

- Write problem goal sheets and develop treatment plans.

- Re-evaluate at appropriate intervals complete home care measures prior to patient discharge.

- Supervise COTA with weekly treatment review.

- Participate in Rehabilitation Unit Planning Committee.

- Schedule LSR patients, coordinating with other disciplines.

- Participate in patient/family conferences; educate family prior to patient discharge.

- Supervise occupational therapy student interns; develop student programs.

- Document daily and weekly patient progress.

- Communicate with other disciplines during and outside conferences.

EDUCATION
BS Degree, Occupational Therapy, 1980
Colorado State University, Ft. Collins, CO

Registered Occupational Therapist
American Occupational Therapy Association

PREVIOUS EMPLOYMENT HISTORY
Occupational Therapist, University Hospital, Denver, CO   1983-85
Occupational Therapist, UC Medical Center, Denver, CO   1980-83
Occupational Therapist Intern, Respite Care, Ft. Collins, CO   1982-85

HEATHER PAULINA MAPLETON
3429 Colina Court
Ft. Collins, CO 80526
(303) 225-0004

OBJECTIVE
An Occupational Therapist position for a private practice

PROFESSIONAL EXPERIENCE
OCCUPATIONAL THERAPIST   1989-Present
CU Medical Center, Denver, CO
- Implement a therapy program working with fine motor skills and upper extremities with recommendations from supervising therapist, administrators and medical staff.
- Organize therapy, instruct activities and encourage client and family participation.
- Apply therapy techniques, observe and record individuals' progress.
- Observe/interpret individual reactions to therapy and prepare reports of progress.
- Assist in professional in-service training programs and training programs for aides.
- Select techniques and methods to help the client regain physical, mental, and/or emotional stability based on goals specified by staff recommendations.
- Conduct evaluation tests, record individual progress, and attend treatment review conferences with other members of the treatment team.
- Work in close cooperation with other disciplines and community services and resources to meet needs of clients.
- Maintain client records and document reports.
- Develop and implement specific therapy treatment and instruction plans.
- Assist in supervising allied health students, medical students, residents, and interns in clinical locations or program areas; assist therapy assistants and volunteers.

PROFESSIONAL PROFILE
- Knowledge of the causes and effects of physical and mental disability and the manifestations and methods of treatment.
- Thoroughly knowledgeable of the methods of teaching and demonstrating techniques of the profession to therapy assistants and other health care personnel.
- Ability to stimulate the interest of clients in a program.
- Skilled at establishing and maintaining effective working relationships with all types of people.

EDUCATION
BS Degree, Occupational Therapy
Colorado State University
Ft. Collins, Colorado, 1989

Registered Occupational Therapist
American Occupational Therapy Association

ROSE R. COHEN
2397 Sandy Lane
Centralia, WA 98531
(206) 330-1298

OBJECTIVE
A Staff Occupational Therapist position

CURRENT PROFESSIONAL EXPERIENCE

PROVIDENCE HOSPITAL, Centralia, WA   1987-present
Staff Occupational Therapist
- Evaluate and assess dysfunction in a variety of diagnoses for all age groups in the rehabilitation department of the hospital.

- Plan and carry out treatment based on established goals for patient care.

- Coordinate objectives and consult with professionals for ongoing patient care.

- Educate patients and families on how to do therapy at home.

- Chart patients' progress on a daily basis.

- Write formalized evaluations on patient performance, progress and ability.

- Verbally report patient treatment to other disciplines during daily treatment.

- Fabricate individualized splints, adaptive equipment, and tool modifications.

- Attend and participate in weekly occupational therapy staff meetings.

- Supervise student interns.

EDUCATION
BS Degree Occupational Therapy, 1983
Colorado State University, Ft. Collins, CO

Registered Occupational Therapist
American Occupational Therapy Association

PREVIOUS EMPLOYMENT HISTORY
Occupational Therapist, Poudre Valley Hospital, Ft. Collins, CO   1983-87
Occupational Therapy Intern, Respite Care, Ft. Collins, CO   1979-83

MARIA ANNA SALVADOR
321 Church Hill Road
Wheat Ridge, CO 80033
(303) 425-2229

OBJECTIVE
An Occupational Therapy Assistant position

CURRENT PROFESSIONAL EXPERIENCE

CERTIFIED OCCUPATIONAL THERAPY ASSISTANT   1989-present
Lutheran Medical Center, Wheat Ridge, CO
- Provide individualized patient treatments (birth-adult) to meet specific goals.

- Set goals and plan for D/C with primary patients.

- Attend and participate in weekly meetings with registered occupational therapist to review and update treatments and goals.

- Document patient progress, status, and outcome as part of the occupational therapy team.

- Communicate with team and family about patient status.

- Learn new techniques/modalities to use with patient.

- Gained valuable knowledge of various diagnoses and precautions in occupational therapy treatment.

EDUCATION
Occupational Therapy Assistant
Pueblo Community College
Pueblo, CO; Certified, 1989

Medical Assistant Program
Medical Careers Training Center
Ft. Collins, CO; Certified 1984

PREVIOUS EMPLOYMENT HISTORY
Home Management, Ft. Collins, CO   1986-89
Medical Assistant, Colorado Rehabilitation Ctr, Pueblo, CO   1984-86
Medical Assistant, Colorado Youth Clinic, Ft. Collins, CO   1975-84

CLIFFORD JAY RAYMOND
3428 Orchard Park
Ft. Collins, CO 80523
(303) 225-0023

OBJECTIVE
A Hospital Staff Pharmacist position.

CURRENT PROFESSIONAL EXPERIENCE

POUDRE VALLEY HOSPITAL, Ft. Collins, CO   1986-present
Staff Pharmacist

- Fill prescriptions while screening for allergies, drug interactions and contradictions.

- Label prescriptions appropriately including precautions.

- Counsel patient as to proper drug use, precautions and adverse reactions.

- Provide drug information and recommendations to physicians, nurses and other health personnel.

- Monitor drug therapy for therapeutic effectiveness and adverse reactions.

- Provide educational programs for patients and health care professionals.

- Keep abreast of new development in drug therapy by attending classes, seminars and reading the latest books and magazines.

- Supervise technicians to assure an accurate drug delivery system.

- Keep accurate records on the acquisition and dispensing of narcotics.

- Check inventory to assure drugs are not expired and are available when needed.

EDUCATION
BS Degree, Pharmacy, 1979
University of Colorado
School of Pharmacy, Boulder, CO

AA Degree, General Studies, 1976
Front Range Community College, Westminster, CO

PREVIOUS EMPLOYMENT HISTORY
Staff Pharmacist, UC Medical Center, Denver, CO   1979-86
Pharmacy Technician, Boulder Drug Store, Boulder, CO   1977-79

RALPH CHARLES BARNEY
2091 Olive Street
Delta, CO 81416
(303) 874-0094

OBJECTIVE
A Hospital Staff Pharmacist position

CURRENT PROFESSIONAL EXPERIENCE

STAFF PHARMACIST   1987-present
Delta County Memorial Hospital, Delta, CO

- Insure that proper medications are dispensed to the patient within state and federal law and regulations for controlled substances.

- Review new doctor orders and make a daily review of medicines for each patient.

- Formulate central and peripheral TPN as requested.

- Check technicians work prior to patient receiving products.

- Screen profiles for allergies and duplication of prescriptions.

- Monitor for more cost saving therapy that is equally effective.

- Complete at least six hours of ACPE per year to keep up with the release of new medicines and constant updating of information.

- Make sure patient medicines in hospital have proper identification.

- Monitor drugs for proper stocking level and storage.

EDUCATION
BS Degree, Pharmacy, 1980
University of Colorado
School of Pharmacy, Boulder, CO

AA Degree, General Studies, 1971
Front Range Community College
Westminster, CO

PREVIOUS EMPLOYMENT HISTORY
Staff Pharmacist, Providence Hospital Centralia, Centralia, WA   1982-87
Staff Pharmacist, UC Medical Center, Denver, CO   1980-82

ASHLEY T. CRUTHERS
1256 Mathews Street
Boulder, CO 85721
(303) 872-4444

OBJECTIVE
Pharmacy Technician for a Hospital

EDUCATION
BA Degree, Communication Studies, 1975
University of Colorado, Boulder, CO

Semester at Sea Program, Summer 1970
University of Pittsburgh
Around the world studies (12 countries)

RELATED PROFESSIONAL EXPERIENCE

BOULDER COMMUNITY COMMUNITY HOSPITAL, Boulder, CO   1980-85
Pharmacy Technician
- In charge of work flow for 16 technicians in the pharmacy department of a busy 6-floor, 400 + bed hospital.
- Key member in converting manual procedures to a highly sophisticated computerized pharmacy system.
  - Developed effective training methods for staff members.
  - Organized/conducted training sessions for technicians and pharmacists.
- Prepared/distributed unit dose & intravenous drugs for all nursing units.
- Interpreted and clarified physicians' orders with attention to detail.
- Served as liaison between pharmacists, physicians and nurses to insure accuracy and safety of pharmaceutical procedures for patients.
- Worked on multiple projects simultaneously under highly pressured situations and consistently met strict deadline schedules.

FT COLLINS PLAZA DRUG, Ft Collins, CA   1970-80
Pharmacy Technician
- Answered customer inquiries and developed a large personal customer base, demonstrating thorough product knowledge and excellent customer service.
- Typed prescriptions into the computer. Thoroughly familiar with medical terminology.
- Prepared claims for Medi-Cal and Health Net insurance customers.
- Maintained purchasing, inventory/quality control, cash management, filing and phone skills with ability to work well under pressure situations in a professional and concerned manner.

PREVIOUS EXPERIENCE
Home Management, Research, Study, Boulder, CO   1985-present
Pharmacy Technician, Paradise Drug, Paradise, CA   1968-70

MELISSA S. SANDSTONE
2349 Kittery Court
Ft. Collins, CO 80525
(303) 224-3009

OBJECTIVE
A Phlebotomist position

PROFESSIONAL EXPERIENCE

POUDRE VALLEY HOSPITAL, Ft. Collins, CO   1989-present
Phlebotomy Technologist
- Obtain blood specimens from infants, children and adult in- and outpatients with accuracy and minimal discomfort.

- Route lab specimens to the correct department or outside lab.

- Ensure the proper handling of all specimens, both in-house and outside hospital including the prevention of infectious contamination to self and others.

- Answer phones, responding promptly, politely and accurately.

- Enter outpatients' data into the computer.

- Set up cultures and prepare slide for microbiology technician.

HUMANA HOSPITAL, Aurora, CO   1987-89
Phlebotomy Laboratory Assistant
- Draw blood from patients.

- Label specimens and log them into the computer system.

- Process sendouts of specimens to go to other labs.

- Call reports in to hospital floors and to private physician offices.

- Direct and answer questions of people who come into the lab.

- Print computerized ward report and deliver to appropriate departments.

EDUCATION
Certified Phlebotomy Technician, 1987
Medical Careers Training Center
Ft. Collins, CO

RANDY ANSIL UHLRICH
3215 Horsetooth Road
Ft. Collins, CO 80526
(303) 223-0094

OBJECTIVE
A Phlebotomist position

CURRENT PROFESSIONAL EXPERIENCE

CERTIFIED PHLEBOTOMY TECHNICIAN   1987-present
Porter Memorial Hospital, Denver, CO
- Collect specimens for in- and out-patients and process for testing; spin down blood, measure urine.

- Gather throat swabs for culture.

- Set up microbiology cultures.

- Log specimens and out-patients onto the computer.

- Process lab paper work including out-patient charts.

- Communicate with doctors, patients and their families.

- Draw legal blood alcohols and testify in court.

- Pick up specimen from the offices of private doctors.

EDUCATION
Certified Phlebotomy Technician, 1985
Medical Careers Training Center
Ft. Collins, CO

PREVIOUS EMPLOYMENT HISTORY
Laboratory Technician, Denver General Hospital, Denver, CO   1986-87
Laboratory Assistant, Boulder Community Hospital, Boulder, CO   1985-86
Volunteer Aide, Avista Hospital, Louisville, CO   1984-85

JUNE S. WASHINGTON
1200 Colfax Lane
Denver, CO 80012
(303) 695-0032

OBJECTIVE
A Physical Therapist position

CURRENT PROFESSIONAL EXPERIENCE

HUMANA HOSPITAL, Aurora, CO   1987-present
Physical Therapist

- Examine/assess patients regarding physical disability, bodily malfunction and pain.

- Outline treatment program and goals to correct, alleviate or limit physical disability.

- Carry out treatment plan to include use of physical agents, measurement of activities and special equipment.

- Prepare accurate written report of patient to include initial evaluation, progress notes and discharge summary.

- Establish special equipment needs and /or adaptive devices; assist patient with proper selection.

- Educate patient and family or caretaker on therapy exercises to do at home and use of special equipment.

- Prepare paperwork for charges including insurance and Medicare forms.

- Communicate progress to physician, vocational counselors, schools or anyone involved in patient's care.

- Assist with orientation and educate new staff and student interns with hospital physical therapy program which includes the latest techniques.

EDUCATION
BS Degree, Physical Therapist, 1983
University of Colorado
Health Science Center, Denver, CO

PREVIOUS EMPLOYMENT HISTORY
Physical Therapist, Porter Memorial Hospital, Denver, CO   1985-87
Physical Therapist, University Hospital, Denver, CO   1983-85

MARTHA W. MATHEWS
1211 W. Mulberry
Ft. Collins, CO 80521
(303) 223-1124

OBJECTIVE
A Physical Therapist position for a private practice

PROFESSIONAL EXPERIENCE

PHYSICAL THERAPIST   1989-Present
UC Denver Medical Center, Denver, CO
- Implement a therapy program working with gross motor skills and lower extremities with recommendations from supervising therapist, administrators and medical staff.
- Organize therapy, instruct activities and encourage client and family participation.
- Apply therapy techniques, observe and record individual progress.
- Observe/interpret individual reactions to therapy and prepare reports of progress.
- Assist in professional inservice training programs and training programs for aides.
- Select techniques and methods to help the client regain physical, mental, and/or emotional stability based on goals specified by staff recommendations.
- Conduct evaluation tests, record individual progress, and attend treatment review conferences with other members of the treatment team.
- Work in close cooperation with other disciplines and community services and resources to meet needs of clients.
- Maintain client records and document reports.
- Develop and implement specific therapy treatment and instruction plans.
- Assist in supervising allied health students, medical students, residents, and interns in clinical locations or program areas; assist therapy assistants and volunteers.

PROFESSIONAL PROFILE
- Knowledge of the causes and effects of physical and mental disability and the manifestations and methods of treatment.
- Thoroughly knowledgeable of the methods of teaching and demonstrating techniques of the profession to therapy assistants and other health care personnel.
- Ability to stimulate the interest of clients in a program.
- Skilled at establishing and maintaining effective working relationships with all types of people.

EDUCATION
BS Degree, Physical Therapy
University of Colorado
Denver, Colorado, 1989

Licensed Physical Therapist
Colorado State Board of Physical Therapy

DIANA JOANNE MARSH
2135 City Park Drive
Ft. Collins, CO 80524
(303) 223-0002

OBJECTIVE
A Physical Therapist Assistant position

CURRENT PROFESSIONAL EXPERIENCE

CERTIFIED PHYSICAL THERAPY ASSISTANT   1986-present
Poudre Valley Hospital, Ft. Collins, CO
- Provide quality treatment to patients at birth through age five.

- Educate patient and family on exercise treatments to practice at home.

- Schedule weekly physical therapy sessions for LSR patients.

- Maintain and update therapists and nursing Labor and Delivery Program files.

- Record daily Quality Assurance statistics for IP/OP in patient department.

- Organize and plan weekly inservices for the physical therapy department.

- Provide patient and family with sources to borrow or purchase special equipment.

- Maintain equipment for units used on labor and delivery units.

- Participate in patient/family conferences with LSR.

- Serve as primary physical therapist coordinator in the absence of department PT.

EDUCATION
Physical Therapist Assistant
Pueblo Community College, Pueblo, CO
Certified, 1986

BA Degree, Physical Education, 1980
University of California at Los Angeles
California Teaching Credential- Multiple Subject

PREVIOUS EMPLOYMENT HISTORY
Phys. Ed. Instructor, Valley College, Van Nuys, CA   1984-86
Softball Coach, Westwood Softball Association, Westwood, CA   1982-84
Student Health Services Coordinator, UCLA, Westwood, CA   1980-82

CAROL SUSAN VANGI
3219 Robertson Street
Denver, CO 80210
(303) 778-0034

OBJECTIVE
A Physical Therapist Assistant position

CURRENT PROFESSIONAL EXPERIENCE

CERTIFIED PHYSICAL THERAPIST ASSISTANT   1987-present
Denver General Hospital, Denver, CO
- Transport patients to and from the rehabilitation therapy unit.

- Assist therapist with lifting, ambulating and isolating patients.

- Prepare sterile set up for burns and isolations.

- Take patients to the bathroom while in the rehabilitation department.

- Clean, sterilize and set up tables.

- Apply pulleys at doctor's request.

- Take special equipment to the floor when assisting patients with treatment.

- Maintain inventory, order supplies and run errands.

- Perform closing of department duties including keeping track of special equipment.

EDUCATION
Certified Physical Therapy Assistant, 1984
Pueblo Community College
Pueblo, CO

PREVIOUS EMPLOYMENT HISTORY
Physical Therapist Assistant, Porter Memorial Hospital, Denver, CO   1986-87

Teacher's Aide, Harris Elementary School, Ft. Collins, CO   1984-86

Hospital Volunteer, Poudre Valley Hospital, Ft. Collins, CO   1982-84

AILYA DEANNE ELISE
1290 Lucy Court
Ft. Collins, CO 80525
(303) 225-0002

OBJECTIVE
A Quality Assurance Assistant position

PROFESSIONAL EXPERIENCE

POUDRE VALLEY HOSPITAL, Ft. Collins, CO   1985-present
Quality Assurance Assistant

- Screen 1100 dismissals per month applying both generic and specific (per medical specialty) criteria, including Tissue Review.

- Prepare monthly monitoring reports for the medical staff based on these findings.

- Compile data and have medical records available to physicians for special studies and coordinate timely retrieval of records for all audits.

- Maintain all documentation pertaining to medical staff quality assurance activities in coded form and locked files in the MRD.

- Keep files of incident reports and pattern the results at end of month to provide statistical information to medical departments, MCE and QA/RM committees.

- Coordinate and schedule third party payor billing audits, gathering information from all ancillary services involved in the care of patient.

- Maintain physician quality assurance peer review files and files on provisional medical staff members for review by their preceptors at the time of appointment.

- Prepare required State reports on patients receiving ECT.

- Update and maintain list of approved abbreviations used at hospital to ensure that we meet JCAR requirements on uniformity.

- Monitor gross spelling errors on transcribed reports, reporting to the head transcriber every 2-3 months.

- Present a confidentiality segment at new employee orientation sessions in the absence of the administrative assistant.

EDUCATION
Registered Records Technician, 1985
Arapahoe Community College, Littleton, CO

ROSLYN J. JEFFRIES
1112 Roserich Street
Denver, CO 80201
(303) 893-9995

OBJECTIVE
A Quality Assurance/Medical Records Assistant

CURRENT PROFESSIONAL EXPERIENCE

QUALITY ASSURANCE ASSISTANT
Porter Memorial Hospital, Denver, CO   1989-present
• Coordinate quality assurance between medical staff and Medical Records.

• Attend all weekly audit committee meetings, take notes, compile information and compose correspondence resulting from each audit meeting.

• Serve as liaison between each audit committee meeting and prepare agendas.

• Perform medical records review on members of medical staff who are up for reappointment.

• Facilitate the allied health professional appointment and reappointment process.

• Provide physician referrals to the public.

• Compose the medical staff calendar on a monthly basis.

• Provide backup support to the medical staff coordinator and other QA assistants.

• Input physician continuing education hours into the MIIS computer system.

• Answer numerous informational questions asked by the hospital staff, other medical professionals and the general public.

EDUCATION
Registered Records Technician, 1987
Arapahoe Community College, Littleton, CO

PREVIOUS EMPLOYMENT HISTORY
Quality Assurance Assistant, University Hospital, Denver, CO   1987-89
Administrative Assistant, UC Medical Center, Denver, CO   1984-87
Medical Secretary, Ft. Collins Youth Clinic, Ft. Collins, CO   1980-84

RUTH B. GREENBAUM
1091 Fairview Court
Ft. Collins, CO 80522
(303) 224-0004

OBJECTIVE
A Quality Assurance Coordinator position

CURRENT PROFESSIONAL EXPERIENCE

POUDRE VALLEY HOSPITAL, Ft. Collins, CO   1988-present
Quality Assurance Coordinator
- Read progress notes and improve the quality and consistency of care given by all disciplines in the hospital.

- Evaluate Medicare and review cases as required by the State of Colorado.

- Schedule and attend Quality Assurance and UR Committee meetings; compile and evaluate reports and implement changes.

- Establish needs and coordinate inservices for staff.

- Supervise volunteer auditing staff; attend audits, report, and implement changes.

- Evaluate all denials and send to Medicare appeals.

- Supervise monthly billing compliance review and assist staff with corrections.

- Audit personnel records annually, assuring they are in compliance with State of Colorado rules and regulations.

- Assist personnel in orienting new staff members.

EDUCATION
Medical Records Administrator, 1984
Regis College, Denver, CO

BS, Nursing, 1975
University of Northern Colorado
Greeley, Colorado

PREVIOUS EMPLOYMENT HISTORY
Quality Assurance Assistant, Porter Memorial Hospital, Denver, CO   1984-88
Staff Nurse, Humana Hospital, Aurora, CO   1980-84
Staff Nurse, Vail Valley Medical Center, Vail, CO   1975-80

JACKI SUE SWANSON
4432 Colfax Avenue
Denver, CO 80262
(303) 458-2229

OBJECTIVE
A Radiologic Technologist position

CURRENT PROFESSIONAL EXPERIENCE

LUTHERAN MEDICAL CENTER, Wheat Ridge, CO   1988-present
Radiologic Technologist
- Perform diagnostic imaging using standard equipment, portable machines and other highly sophisticated machines.

- Position and immobilize patient; determine which equipment would work best.

- Practice radiation protection for patient, co-workers and myself.

- Calculate exposure factors, compensating when necessary and evaluate radiographs for technical quality.

- Assume physical/psychological care for patient during transport and in department.

- Practice aseptic care and recognize/initiate life support measures when needed.

- Assist physicians with imaging procedures and administration of contrast media.

- Obtain information from patient to aid radiologist in evaluating radiographs.

- Obtain early AM portable radiographs as ordered in ICU, CCU and nursery.

- Maintain a good rapport with all departments demonstrating team work while being as efficient as possible.

EDUCATION
AAS Degree, Radiography Program, 1984
Mesa College, Grand Junction, CO

Registered Radiologic Technologist
American Registry of Radiologic Technologists (ARRT)

PREVIOUS EMPLOYMENT HISTORY
Radiologic Technologist, Children's Hospital, Denver, CO   1984-87
Clinical Lab Tech Intern, General Hospital, Denver, CO   1983-84

KELLY RAE BRONSON
5679 Kent Street
Denver, CO 80220
(303) 893-0001

OBJECTIVE
Chief Radiologic Technologist

CURRENT PROFESSIONAL EXPERIENCE

CHIEF RADIOLOGIC TECHNOLOGIST   1985-present
Denver General Hospital, Denver, CO
- Supervise radiology staff including NM, US, CT and Breast Diagnostic Center, Diagnostic Radiology and clerical personnel.

- Assign staff to equipment and procedures including student assignments.

- Provide orientation to new staff members.

- Schedule inservice education, apply for evidence of continuing education and maintain staff records.

- Coordinate quality control and evaluate staff on a regular basis.

- Schedule daily staff workload as well as holidays and vacations.

- Maintain inventory control and purchase supplies.

- Assist director with budget and provide input on purchasing new equipment.

- Recommend new policies and procedures.

- Help resolve problems and disputes with patients, doctors and other technologists.

EDUCATION
AAS Degree, Radiology, 1979
Community College of Denver, Denver, CO

Registered Radiologic Technologist
American Registry of Radiologic Technologists (ARRT)

PREVIOUS EMPLOYMENT HISTORY
Radiologic Technologist, Rose Medical Center, Denver, CO   1983-85
Radiologic Technologist, Routt Memorial Hospital, Steamboat Springs, CO 1981-83
Assistant Lab Technologist, University Hospital, Denver, CO   1979-81

IRA S. JACOBS
2365 19th Avenue
Denver, CO 80218
(303) 458-2210

OBJECTIVE
A Director of Radiology position

CURRENT PROFESSIONAL EXPERIENCE
UNIVERSITY HOSPITAL, Denver, CO   1975-present
Director of Radiology

- Hire, evaluate/review staff; prepare departmental budgets with strict deadlines.

- Provide high quality patient care including the Quality Assurance Program.

- Implement responsibilities for radiology personnel and patient records.

- Generate reports for the Radiology Department.

- Make recommendations for purchases of equipment and negotiate prices.

- Recommend short to long term department goals and implement those approved.

- Coordinate activities from the Radiology Department to other departments.

- Help maintain the quality control of patient's daily examination.

- Ensure that the Radiology Department complies with all Colorado State governmental agency standards, rules, and regulations.

EDUCATION
MBA, Business Administration, 1974
Stanford University, San Francisco, CA

BS Degree, Physics, 1971
University of California, Santa Barbara, CA

Radiologic Technology, 1969
Mesa College, Grand Junction, CO

PREVIOUS EMPLOYMENT HISTORY
Assistant Administrator, General Hospital, San Jose, CA   1973-75
Radiologic Technologist, Memorial Hospital, Colorado Springs, CO   1971-73

DOROTHY L. JOHNSON
131 Briarwood Drive
Los Angeles, CA 90045
(213) 221-8888

Objective: A Recreational Therapist position

**PROFESSIONAL
EXPERIENCE**

1987-92

RECREATIONAL THERAPIST
<u>LA Stroke Activity Center</u>, Santa Monica, CA
- Developed, implemented and supervised community based professional recreation program for stroke victims.
- Assessed, documented and educated patients on appropriate treatment plan.
- Trained and supervised volunteers.
- Prepared monthly newsletter.

1985-87

ACTIVITY SPECIALIST
<u>Northwest Adult Day Care Center</u>, Eugene, OR
- Organized weekend activity program for adults with Alzheimer's Disease.

1982-85

ACTIVITY ASSISTANT
<u>Hillside Heights Convalescent Center</u>, Eugene, OR
- Assisted in planning and implementing recreational activities for long-term care facility for the elderly.

1980-82

RECREATION THERAPY ASSISTANT
<u>Santa Clara Valley Medical Center</u>, Santa Clara, CA
- Assisted in implementing the therapeutic recreation service to individuals with spinal cord injuries for a regional hospital-based rehabilitation center.

EDUCATION

MS Degree, Therapeutic Recreation, 1987
University of Oregon, Eugene, OR

**PROFESSIONAL
PROFILE**

- Specialize in stroke rehab and recreation service to the elderly.
- Possess warmth, patience and a desire to help the disabled.
- Developed a high degree of ingenuity and imagination with good physical coordination to participate in activities.
- Special skills in research, assessment, program design, evaluation and arts and crafts.

JUDITH TANYA LAUGHLIN
2901 Robertson Avenue
Ft. Collins, CO 80524
(303) 224-9995

OBJECTIVE
A Recreational Therapist position

CURRENT PROFESSIONAL EXPERIENCE
POUDRE VALLEY HOSPITAL, Ft. Collins, CO   1981-present
Recreational Therapist

- Schedule, conduct and supervise skilled recreational, educational and therapeutic client services on an acute care, inpatient, 11 bed psychiatric unit.

- Develop written treatment plans of structured activities to meet client needs for long and short term goals.

- Assess each patient on admission and obtain leisure history through intake.

- Participate and observe in development of team cohesiveness.

- Observe and record in chart, reactions and changes in physical and emotional condition; report to staff.

- Provide leisure education on individual and group basis; develop goals for discharge of patient.

- Observe and record patient social skills, attention span, attitudes and interest of each activity.

- Prepare annual recreational therapy budget; monitor budget with a monthly ledger.

- Maintain appropriate interpersonal relationships with patients and staff.

- Make appropriate notations for billing purposes; fill out purchase requests.

EDUCATION
MS Degree, Therapeutic Recreation, 1981
University of Oregon, Eugene, OR

PREVIOUS EMPLOYMENT HISTORY
Recreational Therapist, North Colorado Medical Center, Greeley, CO   1982-85
Rehabilitation Counselor, Eugene Medical Center, Eugene, OR   1981-82

DOROTHY D. LUNDQUIST
1980 Pitkin Road
Ft. Collins, CO 80524
(303) 223-2345

OBJECTIVE
A Respiratory Therapy Technician Supervisor position

PROFESSIONAL PROFILE
- Skilled in the performance of respiratory therapy procedures.
- Thoroughly familiar with the use and application of ventilators.
- Hands-on knowledge of sterilization and aseptic procedures as well as preparing, delivering and troubleshooting respiratory therapy equipment and supplies.
- Demonstrated ability to supervise and administer respiratory therapy treatments according to procedures and policies.
- Act quickly and administer proper therapy in an emergency situation.
- Design and supervise special job assignments.
- Establish and maintain effective working relationships with others.

PROFESSIONAL EXPERIENCE

DENVER MEDICAL CENTER   1987-92
Respiratory Therapy Technician II
- Schedule, supervise and review work performed by other respiratory therapy technicians and assistants.
- Adjust work schedules to meet departmental demands.
- Analyze and resolve operational problems, maintaining quality control and sterilization surveillance programs.
- Purchase all departmental supplies.
- Consult with respiratory therapy supply salesmen and perform quality checks on new equipment.
- Assist in the selection of new employees.
- Help in the preparation of departmental budget.
- Participate in educating patients.
- Maintain and deliver respiratory therapy equipment.
- Assist with bronchoscopies.
- Troubleshoot ventilators.

EDUCATION

AAS Degree, Respiratory Care, 1988
Front Range Community College, Westminster, CO
Certified by the National Board for Respiratory Therapy

JANICE LEAH LAWRENCE
234 Whitcomb Avenue
Ft. Collins, CO 80521
(303) 223-0009

OBJECTIVE
A Respiratory Therapist Technician II position

PROFESSIONAL EXPERIENCE

RESPIRATORY THERAPY TECHNICIAN I
General Hospital, Ft. Collins, CO   1988-present
- Administer intermittent positive pressure breathing treatment, oral and tracheal suction and medications prescribed by a physician.
- Check the operation of inhalation therapy equipment on wards and make necessary adjustments.
- Clean, maintain, and deliver respiratory therapy equipment.
- Assist with repair, maintenance, and sterilization of inhalation therapy equipment.
- Participate in patient education.
- Assist with on-the-job training of respiratory equipment aides.
- Note problems or modifications needed in therapy and reports to coordinator.
- Perform quality control checks of respiratory equipment by culturing items on shelf and in use.
- Check and record patient progress; keep records and prepare reports.
- Function as lead worker with diplomacy and tact in the supervisor's absence.

PROFESSIONAL PROFILE
- Gained considerable knowledge of inhalation therapy agents and the effects of inhalation therapy agents on the human body.
- Thorough knowledge of inhalation therapy theory and practice.
- Act quickly and administer proper therapy in an emergency situation.
- Design and supervise special job assignments.
- Establish and maintain effective working relationships with others.
- Skilled in administering a variety of inhalation therapy treatments.

EDUCATION
AAS Degree, Respiratory Care, 1988
Front Range Community College, Westminster, CO
Certified by the National Board for Respiratory Therapy

ROSALIE GADOS
3412 Cherry Creek Road
Aurora, CO 80014
(303) 693-1110

OBJECTIVE
A Medical Social Worker position.

CURRENT PROFESSIONAL EXPERIENCE
SOCIAL WORKER   1986-present
Centennial Peaks Hospital, Louisville, CO

- Assist acute, chronic, terminal illness, disabled, pregnancy/childbirth patients with psychological, social and emotional needs while adjusting to health issues.

- Coordinate and implement discharge planning services for hospital patients.

- Participate in discharge planning rounds and patient care conferences.

- Provide direct counseling service to individuals, families and groups.

- Evaluate psychosocial functioning of patients and families.

- Provide staff consultation regarding patient care issues.

- Organize patient care services for out-patient pediatrics program.

- Develop and implement new programs, policies, and procedures related to psychosocial care of patients.

- Provide patient/staff education through scheduled inservices and group meetings.

- Participate in community programs and hospital board meetings that relate to health care needs on social problems in the community at large.

EDUCATION
BA Degree, Sociology, 1980
University of California, Santa Barbara, CA

AA Degree, General Studies, 1978
Front Range Community College, Westminster, CO

PREVIOUS EMPLOYMENT HISTORY
Social Worker, Denver General Hospital, Denver, CO   1982-86
Social Service Coordinator, UC Medical Center, Denver, CO   1980-82
Clerk, Jefferson County Social Services, Denver, CO   1979-80

MARK NICHOLAS RAFFY
3290 Smith Street
Ft. Collins, CO 80524
(303) 224-5594

OBJECTIVE
Supervisor of Special Procedures in the Radiology Department

CURRENT PROFESSIONAL EXPERIENCE

SPECIAL PROCEDURES SUPERVISOR   1988-present
Poudre Valley Hospital (Radiology Dept), Ft. Collins, CO
- Supervise radiology personnel in CT/ANGIO, including staff evaluation, scheduling, quality control insuring a smooth flow of patients through the CT/ANGIO area.
- Perform CAT SCANs and ANGIO Graphic studies.
- Provide emergency on-call assistance for CT/ANGIO.
- Deliver quality control procedures for all CAT SCANs and ANGIO studies.
- Orientate and train all new CT/ANGIO technicians.
- Administer oral and IV contrast agents for entire department.
- Maintain inventory control and departmental purchase supplies.
- Recommend and implement new and revised policies, procedures and regulations.
- Assist administrative technologist with budgetary duties in the CT/ANGIO area.
- Provide information for equipment maintenance.
- Maintain accurate patient records.
- Follow up on all ANGIOs and CTs.

EDUCATION
AAS Degree, Radiography, 1980
Community College of Denver

Registered Radiologic Technologist
American Registry of Radiologic Technologists (ARRT)

PREVIOUS EMPLOYMENT HISTORY
X-ray Technologist, Denver General Hospital, Denver, CO   1986-88
Radiologic Technologist, Swedish Hospital, Denver, CO   1984-86
Radiologic Technologist, UC Medical Center, Denver, CO   1980-84
Radiology Intern, North Colorado Medical Center, Greeley, CO   1979-80

BRENDA SUE BENTLEY
4802 Howes Street
Greeley, CO 80631
(303) 330-0832

OBJECTIVE
Radiology Special Procedures Technician

CURRENT PROFESSIONAL EXPERIENCE

NORTH COLORADO MEDICAL CENTER, Greeley, CO   1989-present
Special Procedures Technician
- Operate diagnostic, CT and special procedures imaging equipment.

- Position patient.

- Calculate exposure factors.

- Assist physician with administration of contrast media.

- Help physician with imaging procedures and catheterization of arteries.

- Monitor vital signs and initiate life support measures when necessary.

- Evaluate films for technical quality.

- Meet physical/psychological needs of each patient during exams and procedures.

- Rotate on-call schedule; maintain patient records; stock supplies, and clean CT and special procedure areas.

EDUCATION
AAS Degree, Radiography, 1882
Community College of Denver, Denver, CO

Registered Radiologic Technologist
American Registry of Radiologic Technologists (ARRT)

PREVIOUS EMPLOYMENT HISTORY
X-ray Technician, Swedish Medical Center, Denver, CO   1984-86
Radiologic Technician, Denver General Hospital, CO   1982-84

LUCY KATHRYN SCHULTZ
5431 University Drive
Denver, CO 80218
(303) 390-1234

OBJECTIVE
A Speech-Language Pathologist position

CURRENT PROFESSIONAL EXPERIENCE

SPALDING REHABILITATION HOSPITAL, Denver, CO   1989-present
Speech-Language Pathologist

- Perform diagnostic speech and language procedures to children and adults of out-patient, inpatient and home care.

- Develop/administer treatment plans including family education for home programs.

- Document evaluations, treatment, progress and results.

- Develop programs for new services which include protocols, assessment procedures and treatment programs.

- Promote department services through verbal and written distribution of information and staffing booths.

- Consult with physicians, staff and other professionals, family members and patients.

- Participate in inservices, continuing education and professional reading.

- Coordinate services for interdisciplinary teams.

- Present rounds and inservices for staff and community organizations.

EDUCATION
MS Degree, Speech-Language Pathology, 1985
Colorado State University, Ft. Collins, CO

Certificate of Clinical Competence (CCC-SP)
American Speech-Language & Health Association (ASHA)

PREVIOUS EMPLOYMENT HISTORY
Speech-Language Pathologist, University Hospital, Denver, CO   1987-89
Speech-Language Pathologist, Denver Youth Clinic, Denver, CO   1985-87

ADRIAN L. JORDAN
509 Bryandale Way
Ft. Collins, CO 80524
(303) 224-6665

Objective: A Surgical Technologist position

PROFESSIONAL EXPERIENCE

SURGICAL TECHNOLOGIST
Poudre Valley Hospital, Ft. Collins, CO   1988-present
- Developed thorough knowledge and skills with the following surgical procedures: vascular, ophthalmic, cardio-vascular, general, thoracic, plastic, trauma, neuro, orthopedic, urologic and GYN/OB.

- Sterilize instruments implementing aseptic technique and evaluation of equipment safety.

- Participated in a video production of cardio-vascular surgical technique for public broadcasting presently being used for in-patient educational programs.

- Collaborate with hospital staff to provide quality patient care.

CERTIFICATION/AFFILIATION

Certified Surgical Technologist, 1983
Pueblo Community College, Pueblo, CO

Member, Association of Surgical Technologists

PREVIOUS EMPLOYMENT HISTORY

Surgical Technologist
St. Joseph Hospital, Los Angeles, CA   1985-88

Surgical Assistant
Cedar Sinai Hospital, Los Angeles, CA   1983-85

Hospital Aide
Valley Medical Center, Los Angeles, CA   1982-83

WENDY S. ROBINS
2398 Colfax Avenue
Denver, CO 80220
(303) 320-3333

OBJECTIVE
An Ultrasound Technologist position

CURRENT PROFESSIONAL EXPERIENCE

ULTRASOUND TECHNOLOGIST   1986-present
Denver General Hospital, Denver, CO

- Obtain a complete patient history and correlate with other diagnostic procedures on sonogram.

- Evaluate sonograms for technical or photographic quality before presentation to radiologist.

- Practice aseptic technique and perform portable exams on critically ill patients being careful to properly dismantle and move equipment.

- Prepare technologist impression of each exam to review with the radiologist.

- Stock needed supplies and maintain cleanliness of equipment and lab counters.

- Provide technical input for equipment and supply purchase decisions.

- Assume responsibility for portions of departmental quality assurance program.

- Rotate on-call for 24 hour emergency ultrasound exams ordered.

- Apply scanning skills along with in-depth knowledge of soft tissue anatomy and pathophysiology to insure image quality for documented diagnostic information.

EDUCATION
Ultrasound Technologist Certification Program, 1983
Penrose-St. Francis Healthcare System
Colorado Springs, CO

Registered Sonographer/Ultrasound Technologist
American Registry of Diagnostic Medical Sonographers

PREVIOUS EMPLOYMENT HISTORY
Ultrasound Technologist, Poudre Valley Hospital, Ft. Collins, CO   1984-86
Radiology Dept. Intern, St. Joseph Hospital, Denver, CO   1982-83

HARRY JOSEPH JACKSON
345 Noel Drive
Boulder, CO 80302
(303) 490-1234

Objective: An Ultrasound Technologist Supervisor position

PROFESSIONAL EXPERIENCE

ULTRASOUND STAFF TECHNOLOGIST   1982-present
Boulder Memorial Hospital, Boulder, CO
- Perform diagnostic X-ray and ultrasound procedures for abdominal and OB/GYN patients in the Radiology Department of a 100 bed facility.

- Maintain the Quality Assurance program.

- Troubleshoot and repair radiology equipment.

- Schedule payroll, prepare accounts receivable and payable, maintain inventory control and purchase supplies.

- Supervise radiology staff in the absence of the department supervisor.

X-RAY/ULTRASOUND ASSISTANT   1980-82
UC Medical Center, Denver, CO
- Assist technologist with all areas of diagnostic X-ray, ultrasound and CT procedures for abdominal and OB/GYN patients in the Radiology Department.

- Coordinate quality control under the supervision of the staff technician.

EDUCATION

Ultrasound Technologist Certification Program, 1980
University of Colorado, Denver, CO

Registered Sonographer/Ultrasound Technologist
American Registry of Diagnostic Medical Sonographers

> ## Veterinary Specialist I—Functional Resume

ROBERT P. GLENN
8574 Harmony Road
Ft. Collins, CO 80526
(303) 223-0021

OBJECTIVE
A Veterinary Specialist position

PROFESSIONAL EXPERIENCE

Clinical Experience
- Perform maintenance on anesthetic equipment; maintain surgery/anesthetic records.
- Serve as Staff Anesthesiologist during after hour emergencies on an on-call basis.
- Monitor recovery of clinical animals following surgery.
- Implement emergency procedures during critical periods of surgery to sustain life of the animal.
- Collect blood for transfusions; maintain a blood donor program.
- Maintain a supply of inventories, controlled drug logs and rebated files.
- Oversee students during anesthetic induction, maintenance/recovery of animals.
- Insure proper preparation of operating rooms; supervise sterile technique in surgical suites; order surgeries.
- Administer anesthetic agents to large/small animals.

Teaching Experience
- Instruct veterinary students in selecting and administering anesthetic agents for large and small animal clinic cases.
- Provide instruction in the use of volatile vapors and injectable agents, and the use of monitoring equipment such as EKG, CVP and blood pressure transducers.
- Assist in student grading and development of teaching materials such as texts, handouts, slides and videotapes.

Administrative Experience
- Coordinate work schedules and assignments.
- Establish new procedures to maintain a current and efficient surgical department.
- Coordinate supplies and equipment with other hospital sections.
- Initiate action to repair, replace and upgrade hospital equipment.
- Analyze cost of surgical procedures/provide input into section budgeting process.

EDUCATION
Certified Veterinary Technician, 1983
Bel-Rea Institute of Animal Technology, Denver, CO

EMPLOYMENT HISTORY
CSU VETERINARY TEACHING HOSPITAL, Ft. Collins, CO   1983-present
Veterinary Specialist I, (1986-present)
Veterinary Technician, (1983-86)

HENRY R. NOWAK
7896 Horsetooth Road
Ft. Collins, CO 80526
(303) 223-0045

OBJECTIVE
A Veterinary Technician position

CURRENT PROFESSIONAL EXPERIENCE

CSU VETERINARY TEACHING HOSPITAL, Ft. Collins, CO   1987-present
Registered Veterinary Technician
- Instruct junior and senior veterinary students in the principles of aseptic technique and operation room preparation.
- Oversee operating room sterile techniques.
- Teach techniques of the following: scrubbing, gloving, gowning, surgical preparation of the patient and set up of anesthetic machines.
- Coordinate pre-surgery set up of operating rooms with surgical schedule.
- Position patients for small and large animal surgery.
- Clean, reorganize and restock operating rooms immediately after surgery.
- Initiate repairs; replace machines and instruments in the operation room.
- Perform closure of suture orifices and urinary catheterizations.
- Maintain surgery logs and records; order and maintain supplies and equipment.
- Initiate documentation to itemize charges for billing and pharmaceuticals.
- Operate and maintain an Amsco autoclave for flashing contaminated instruments.
- Assess workability and set up of: suction units, Valley Lab Cautery, Bovie cautery, orthopedic drills, surgical lights, hydraulic tables, pneumatic tourniquets, blood pressure monitors and transducers, EKG monitor.

EDUCATION
Certified Veterinary Technician, 1987
Colorado Mountain College
Roaring Fork Campus, Glenwood Springs, CO

PROFESSIONAL PROFILE
- Gained considerable knowledge of animal anatomy and physiology.
- Skilled in the use of surgical instruments, supplies, equipment and aseptic/manipulative techniques.
- Ability to handle, restrain and care for large and small animals.
- Familiar with medical terminology with thorough knowledge of operating room procedures.
- Ability to establish and maintain positive working relationships with clients and all levels of professionals.
- Outstanding ability to communicate subject matter to students in an instructional setting, orally and in writing.

WANDA SUE JOSLYN
2980 Peterson Street
Denver, CO 80204
(303) 629-3332

OBJECTIVE
A Ward Clerk position

CURRENT PROFESSIONAL EXPERIENCE

DENVER GENERAL HOSPITAL, Denver, CO   1988-present
Ward Clerk II

- Type and log in birth certificates; have client check for accuracy and sign; explain legalities as necessary.

- Enter fees into the computer for each baby on a daily basis while maintaining an accurate log of charges.

- Transcribe physician's orders onto Kardex; place orders and ensure that RN is aware of orders.

- Answer busy phones and take messages; set up schedule for tests; order supplies.

- Hand carry specimens to lab and run other errands.

- Gather items needed for baby to transport from various sources; photocopy and organize baby's chart.

- Greet parents and visitors; educate them on hospital visiting procedures.

- Check and relay lab results.

- Organize the nursery to keep things going as smoothly as possible under the most chaotic circumstances.

EDUCATION
AAS Degree, Nursing, in-progress
Front Range Community College
Westminster, CO

PREVIOUS EMPLOYMENT HISTORY
Medical Secretary, Poudre Valley Hospital, Ft. Collins, CO   1985-88
Medical Secretary, University Hospital, Denver, CO   1983-85

RUTH J. CRANE
2109 Robertson Street
Ft. Collins, CO 80524
(303) 224-0043

OBJECTIVE
A Ward Clerk position

CURRENT PROFESSIONAL EXPERIENCE
WARD CLERK II

Poudre Valley Hospital, Ft. Collins, CO   1986-present

- Initiate the necessary tests and nursing care performed on patients by ordering and coordinating tests, documenting medicines and transcribing onto patients' Kardexes.

- Take orders from charts.

- Make sure patients receive correct diet trays.

- Take used equipment to central supply and pick up needed equipment.

- Order daily lab reports.

- Relay new orders and information to nurses.

- Order dietary supplies for the floor and keep unit stocked.

- Type demographic entry for new admissions.

- Ensure all patients have CS charge cards in the Kardex file.

- Communicate with admitting to find out which are pre-op patients and type into computer for next shift staff.

- Log in nurses and progress notes for the following day.

- Answer phones for the Surgical Department.

EDUCATION
Certified Health Care Secretary/Unit Coordinator, 1982
Boulder Valley Voc-Tech Center, Boulder, CO

PREVIOUS EMPLOYMENT HISTORY
Ward Clerk, Denver General Hospital, Denver, CO   1982-86

SUSIE R. WHITNEY
1100 Highland Avenue
Denver, CO 80229
(303) 861-0005

OBJECTIVE
A Secretary position at a hospital

CURRENT PROFESSIONAL EXPERIENCE
WARD SECRETARY   1986-present
<u>Lutheran Medical Center</u>, Wheat Ridge, CO
- Transcribe doctors' and nurses' orders, type into computer and call for stats in the Cardiovascular Department.

- Answer phone system and questions asked in a professional and concerned manner.

- Communicate between doctors, nurses, and patients.

- Keep diet board, discharges and housekeeping up-to-date with admissions.

- Run errands to various hospital departments including taking specimens and blood to the laboratory.

- Instrumental in helping charge nurse select rooms for patients and nursing staff; set up rooms for patients.

- Order labs, EKGs X rays, scans, diets, and treatments through the computer.

SECRETARY   1982-86
<u>Law Offices of Branden & Moyer</u>, Denver, CO
- In charge of office for two attorneys; demonstrated efficiency and confidentiality under pressure situations.

- Typed, edited and finalized legal documents and correspondence on the IBM computer with speed and accuracy.

- Maintained and reconciled bank accounts; dealt with clients in a highly professional and diplomatic manner.

- Answered phones, scheduled appointments and ordered all office supplies.

EDUCATION
Certified Health Care Secretary/Unit Coordinator, 1986
<u>Boulder Valley Voc-Tech Center</u>, Boulder, CO

Index to Resume Samples by Profession